In memory of our co-workers Tanki Mokhele and Mandu Chiloane who have both died tragically since this book was first published. May their creative spirit live on as more and more children experience the magic of art.

# Khula 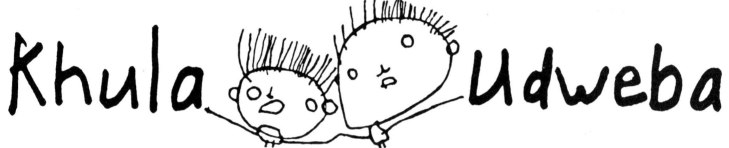 Udweba

## A handbook about teaching art to children

Compiled and written by
Lindy Solomon

Edited by Janet Orlek

NOLWAZI

Design by Charlotte Schaer and Lindy Solomon
Layout and production by Charlotte Schaer
Illustrations by Wandile Mlangeni, Tanki Mokhele, Charlotte Schaer and Sydney Selepe
Photographs of children and teachers at work by Gideon Mendel
Photographs of most of the artworks by Pierre Hinch
Cover photographs of mural at Orlando Children's Home by Pierre Hinch
Cover design by Charlotte Schaer

**Our special thanks to:**

U.S. Aid, for funding the first phase of the Khula Udweba project and the first publication of this book.

The Foundation for the Creative Arts, for a loan which made this second impression possible.

Steven Sack, for initiating the Khula Udweba project and for his ongoing support.

Zakhele Mpalweni, the director of the African Institute of Art, for giving the Khula Udweba project sound direction and for supporting us throughout the making of this book.

Lovell Friedman, who helped write the ceramics section and photographed claywork made by children in workshops at the Community Arts Project and the Touch Gallery in Cape Town.

All those who ran workshops for the Khula Udweba course in their specialised areas of art, history of art, art education, psychology or drama: Linda Ballen, Vanessa Barnett, Gillian Cargill, Mickey Dube, Handspring Puppet Company, Thami Jali, Annette Laubscher, Dumisane Mabaso, David Moteane, Anitra Nettleton, Yvonne Rinaldi. Their ideas have fed directly or indirectly into this book.

All those people who read drafts of the manuscript at various stages and gave valuable comment: Linda Ballen, Stanley Cohen, Lionel Davis, David Koloane, Van Zyl le Grange, Elske Maxwell, Modiegi Morailane, Ruth Sack, Steven Sack, Kim Sacks, Tshidi Sefako, Durant Sihlali, Ronnie Simons, Andrew Steyn.

Gillian Cargill, Adrian Kohler, Annette Laubscher and Justin Mthembu, for contributing a few photographs or illustrations.

First published in 1989
by African Institute of Art
Funda Centre, P O Box 359, Orlando 1804
Soweto, South Africa
Reprinted 1993, 1996, 1997
This edition published 1996 by
Nolwazi Educational Publishers (Pty) Ltd
P O Box 32718
Braamfontein
2017
Gauteng
South Africa

ISBN 1875048 68 5

Repro by Graphic Process and Fotoplate

Printed and bound by CTP Book Printers (Pty) Ltd, Caxton Street, Parow 7500, Cape Town

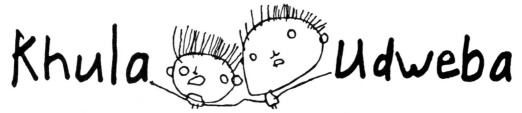

# Khula Udweba

## A handbook about teaching art to children

This book has evolved out of a collective working process in the Khula Udweba project, over the past two years.

All the participants in the first Khula Udweba course contributed their ideas and experiences. The participants are:

**Mandu Chiloane, Thandi Dayel, Dumisani Khumalo, Maggie Makhoana, Nothemba Maqalekane, Wandile Mlangeni, Tanki Mokhele, Helen Sebidi, John Sekhwela, Sydney Selepe, Lindy Solomon (co-ordinator) and Nhlanhla Xaba.**

**The children in the Khula Udweba art groups** created the artworks which are spread throughout the book. Without them, this book could not have been written.

# Contents

# Foreword

The absence of art classes, formal or informal, in the life of most black children in South Africa is a serious denial of a right, necessary for their growth and development. In South Africa, art education is enjoyed by the rich and privileged communities only. But art is important for children in all communities, regardless of race, culture, class or geographic setting.

Children are by nature very creative. It is this strong sense of creativity around which the activities of children rotate. This creativity needs to be captured, guided and developed early in their lives as a base and stimulation for their future learning and growth.

From a very young age, children interpret their impressions spontaneously into images which resemble people, animals and objects of all sorts. For generations past, boys in rural areas found great joy and fulfilment in using clay to make animals of all kinds and neighbourhood scenes. Girls used grass to make dolls, family scenes and a variety of small articles such as bangles, headgear and necklaces. Children also expressed their ideas by drawing on the ground. These young people exploited the materials in their environment in order to express themselves creatively. In this way they communicated their understanding of life around them. Creative activities were part of social and cultural life and were carried down from generation to generation. Many children revealed great talent and some traditional musical instruments and artworks of great beauty have come out of these childlike efforts.

Economic, political, social and cultural pressures from foreign invasion brought about severe changes in black communities. This had a very negative influence on the values and activities of children. The newcomer missionaries and traders interpreted traditional music and dancing as primitive and so denied the beauty of these cultural activities. Lack of natural raw material in the urban townships affected children's creative activities adversely. Efforts by the church and the schools to replace indigenous activities were ineffective and strange to the community. People did not receive satisfaction from these efforts and were not in a position to express their dissatisfaction.

In much later years, schools which introduced "art" encouraged uniformity and conformity, rather than individual spontaneous creativity. The few recreational centres which attempted to promote art in the community made it a commercial venture, rather than an educative process. Many present day educational and recreational centres have created a myth that art education is expensive. But natural materials and throw-aways in the environment and cheap art materials can be used to create art.

The absence of art as a medium of self-expression has left a vacuum in the lives of the majority of growing young children in this community.

The birth of the Khula Udweba project and this book bring hope and great possibilities for young people whose educational opportunities are so limited in the present system.

I had a rare opportunity to observe children at work in one of the Khula Udweba art groups. This experience was both a revelation and an inspiration for me. I was struck by the confidence of those young people as they took their chairs around the table where they were going to work, by the relaxed interaction they had with their teachers and by their determination and uninhibited participation. The whole group enjoyed and took pride in their individual work, without comparing and competing with each other.

The Khula Udweba project places more emphasis on the development of creativity and self-expression than on the final art product. Despite this, some of the children produced very impressive work and might even become professional artists in years to come.

In a community so denied and with so many constraints, exposed to a system of education so sterile and stereotyped, Khula Udweba can begin to define new direction, give new hope and possibly new rewarding opportunities for a brighter future for many youngsters.

I cannot emphasize enough the need and the value that lies in a programme like Khula Udweba. I hope that many people will use this well-prepared book and that it will give direction to those dedicated to the growth and benefit of youth in the community and to the enrichment of all people in South Africa.

Ellen K. Kuzwayo

Soweto 1989

Portrait of Ellen Kuzwayo. Pencil. Age 11. Orlando.

# Introduction

## How this book came about

This book has evolved out of the Khula Udweba project which aims to develop art education for children. The project was set up by the African Institute of Art and is based at Funda Centre in Diepkloof, Soweto. *Khula Udweba* means *draw as you grow* or *grow as you draw*. The Khula Udweba project is founded on the belief that art is vitally important in educating the whole child. Art education helps to create well-balanced children by developing creative thinking, self-confidence and social awareness.

The project was initiated because of the neglect of art education in the majority of schools in this country. Art is seen by the education authorities as a luxury and only a few privileged schools have specialised art teachers and offer art as a subject. In most schools, no art materials are provided and art is regarded as a recreational activity or it is totally ignored. So thousands of children in our communities are not given the opportunity to experience art as a meaningful part of their education.

The Khula Udweba project offers a course for people who want to develop themselves as child art teachers in the community. The project also sets up community-based child art groups so that as many children as possible are given the opportunity to explore art.

As the first group of participants in the Khula Udweba course, we began working together in early 1987. Some members of our group had previous involvement in artmaking, others had none. Some of us had teaching experience of one kind or another, others had never taught before. But we all shared the belief that art is an essential part of children's education.

We have been working together for two years, meeting two afternoons a week for workshops. In these workshops, we did projects to develop our own creativity and understanding of visual art. We learnt practical artmaking skills to use with children and organisational skills to run child art groups. We explored teaching methods and discussed child psychology. Together we aimed to develop a meaningful art programme for children living in the townships where there are limited facilities and resources.

In addition to these workshops, we have each been teaching a regular group of children once a week. In this way, we have involved about three hundred children (aged 5 – 13 years) from Soweto, Katlehong and Alexandra in the first phase of the project. Some of us have set up child art groups, working in church halls, children's homes, community centres, private garages and sometimes even outside. A few of us have been teaching children in existing art centres. Wherever possible, we have encouraged parents to support and involve themselves actively in their children's art programmes. We also aim to educate parents about the role of art in their children's education.

During the Khula Udweba course, we consulted many books about art education for children. We found that most of the available books on child art are produced abroad and are very expensive. Also, most of them assume that the art teacher has well-equipped facilities and a large budget for art materials. We soon realised that there is a need for locally produced books which contextualise art education in South Africa and which can be used in areas which have limited facilities and resources.

So, we decided to document our working process over the past two years in this book. The material for the book has been drawn from our teaching experience in our child art groups, the children's responses and our discussions in workshops and parents' meetings. Most of the artworks in the book have been made by children in the Khula Udweba child art groups during the past two years.

We hope this book will be a useful resource for people working in their communities who want to develop creativity in children. We hope that it is easy to understand and use and that it inspires enthusiasm and confidence in those who are entering the world of child art teaching for the first time.

It is our dream that child art groups will be set up all over the country and that many children will be reached through this book. All children have the right to express themselves creatively — let's work towards creating opportunities for every child to do this!

The taxi. Koki pen. Age 12. Orlando.

## Who can use this book

This book is for everybody interested in teaching children art. You do not have to be an artist or a teacher to use this book, nor do you need lots of money or well-equipped artrooms.

We hope that many of the following people will find this book useful:

- community-based art teachers of children
- cultural workers in youth organisations working with children
- child art teacher trainees in colleges
- teachers who have the opportunity to teach art in class or in extra-mural clubs
- parents who are keen to enrich their children at home
- community workers in crêches and day-care centres
- teenagers who can work in groups without adult supervision

The book is based on our experience of working in urban townships with children aged 5 – 13 years. However, the material can be adapted for different groups and different working contexts e.g. for pre-school children, for adolescents and for groups working in rural areas.

## What this book is about

In this book, we share our approach to teaching children art and we explain how we use various materials and techniques with children.

This book has two parts:

### Part One: Our approach to art teaching

In this section, we give our ideas about why it is important to teach children art and we outline our guiding principles for working with children. We talk about planning a meaningful art programme for children and the importance of choosing relevant subject matter and good motivation methods. We also review the basic elements of art. Finally, we explain how we organise in difficult working conditions and we outline which art techniques and materials we explore with children.

We have included some drawings, mostly by young children (5 – 8 years) and some photographs of our working process.

### Part Two: Art processes and techniques

In Part Two, we explain 36 art techniques that we have used with children. These techniques are grouped into 8 different sections. There is a section for each of the following art processes: drawing, collage, painting, relief printing, sculpture, ceramics, mask-making and puppet-making.

In the introduction to each section, we briefly mention how the art process has been explored in Africa, in the past and today. For each technique, we list which materials are needed and we explain in detail how to teach the technique. We suggest the appropriate age group, as well as the amount of time needed to complete the artworks. We talk about what we have experienced doing each technique with children. We also give some extra ideas for exploring the technique further and suggestions for subject matter.

There are examples of children's artworks for each technique. Most of the examples shown are first attempts at these techniques. Occasionally, we have included some artworks that we have made ourselves during the Khula Udweba course.

## How to use this book

This is not a recipe book with carefully planned projects for you to follow step-by-step. It is a handbook which can guide and help you to teach children art in a meaningful way. We encourage you to use the book thoughtfully and critically and to discuss issues and ideas with others interested in teaching children art. Use the book creatively and flexibly and adapt it to suit your working context.

Here are some guidelines on how to use this book:

■ Read and study Part One about our approach to art teaching thoroughly before you teach any of the techniques in Part Two. You can only use the techniques meaningfully and effectively after you have thought about and explored the issues in Part One fully. We encourage you to refer back to Part One as often as possible, to read sections regularly, to discuss issues with colleagues and to reflect often on your own approach to teaching children art.

■ Before we could structure our art programmes, we had to ask ourselves questions about the children in our groups and about our particular working conditions. We have listed some of these questions on pages 18 and 31. We encourage you to also ask yourself these questions so that you can plan and organise an art programme that is appropriate for your children and your working context.

■ Explore and experiment with as many methods of motivation as possible. Plan carefully how you will motivate the children and refer regularly to the section *Motivating children to create* for ideas on how to vary your methods of motivation.

■ We have suggested some materials for a basic art kit on page 33 but you do not need all of these materials. You should use whatever materials you have in as many ways as possible. You do not need to begin with a fully equipped art kit — you can build up your kit over time. Make sure that you also use found materials from your own environment. Refer to Appendix A for information about buying and collecting materials.

A woman selling mielies. Koki pen. Age 6. Diepkloof.

- When working with children, do not rigidly follow the order of the techniques as they appear in the book. Rather, select particular techniques from each section so that your art programme has variety. Try to create a balance of two-dimensional and three-dimensional techniques.

- It is very important for you to do each technique yourself before you do it with the children. This will give you a chance to experience the process and to discover any potential problems.

- You must read the guidelines for each technique carefully, but this is not enough. It is also essential to read the section *What we have experienced with children* for each technique. There is important information in this section e.g. where to get certain materials and how to care for them, things to watch out for when using the technique with children, etc.

- For each technique, we have given some suggestions for subject matter which is especially suitable. These are not the only possibilities — you should refer to page 19 for other ideas and think of your own ideas.

- Try to expose children to traditional and contemporary art, whenever possible. We mention some relevant art and artists in the introduction to each group of techniques and in some of the sections about our experiences. We encourage you to do further reading about this — refer to the booklist in Appendix D for some useful books about traditional and contemporary art in Africa.

- The examples of children's artworks for each technique are as important as the text. Study them carefully to see how the materials have been used and what effects have been created. Observe how children of different ages have explored the materials and techniques differently. Take care not to use these examples as models and always choose your own subject matter for each technique.

- Prepare your art lessons well in advance so that you can inform children to begin collecting materials, if necessary. You must plan your lessons carefully. You need to decide what the aims of the lesson are, what materials you need, which subject matter you will use, how you will motivate the children and how you will structure the lesson. Use the lesson plan form in Appendix B to help you plan your lessons. You may want to make photocopies of this page so that you can fill in a lesson plan form when you plan each lesson.

- After each lesson, it is useful to evaluate your own teaching, the children's work and whether the project was appropriate for your group. Refer to the evaluation form in Appendix C to help you do this. You may wish to make photocopies of this form for your own use. If you fill in this form after each art lesson, you will have a record of your impressions and experiences for future reference.

- Try to read as many books as possible on art and art education. We have included a list of books which we find useful in Appendix D.

- We have included a glossary, mainly of art terms, in Appendix E. Refer to this glossary when you come across words that you do not understand.

Enjoy the book. Use it creatively!
We welcome your feedback and comments.

Khula Udweba

African Institute of Art. Funda Centre. PO Box 359. Orlando 1804. Soweto.

10

# Part one
# Our approach to art teaching

Woman in traditional Xhosa dress. Koki pen. Age 11. Katlehong.

# Why teach art?

*In the Khula Udweba workshops, we have spent much time discussing the importance of art education and the role of art in society. Here are some of our ideas.*

I have been educated in a system that prepares students mainly for the needs of industry. I feel that our children should not be trapped in the same system. We need to develop alternative education that includes a cultural aspect with subjects like art, music, drama, poetry, dance and creative writing. The education system for blacks in this country ignores the arts as an important part of education. Our children are cut off from creative experience and cultural traditions. If our children are exposed to arts education as early as possible, they will begin to respect their own culture. Education should prepare children to contribute creatively to society, not only to meet the needs of industry. I feel that arts education can help a great deal to develop social and cultural awareness in our children.

*Sydney Selepe*

Children love art because it is a way of expressing their feelings. Most subjects at school do not give them this opportunity. Creative experience stimulates and develops children's imaginations and powers of observation. Art broadens their capacity for love and beauty. The child who expresses himself honestly becomes confident in his own independent thinking – he expresses his own thoughts and ideas in his own way. Through art children can make good friends and develop a sense of humour because they work together and share ideas all the time. In their art, children display their true colours in life and their parents can get to know them very well.

*John Sekhwela*

I am always strongly attracted by the beauty of birds: canaries, budgies, flamingos and the strength of eagles. They present to me the beauty of the child population. These mysterious, pretty, free, loving and trusting individuals are as powerful as eagles and as beautiful as the mentioned birds. These people are part of every community. They spend their time in their homes, schools, early learning centres, clubs, streets and art centres. These multitudes need love, guidance and discipline. They are energetic, spontaneous, expressive and sensitive. Their brains are very absorbent and imaginative. They are open and inventive. These natural qualities can be developed and retained by encouraging children in artmaking.

*Maggie Makhoana*

In our schools today, children are trained to be passive receivers of knowledge. They are not actively involved in their learning and they are not taught to take responsibility for themselves. Children are seldom given a chance to make decisions for themselves so they do not learn decision-making skills. With art education we hope to overcome this problem. We create a free environment in which children work. They learn to become responsible and decisive. When a child asks a question in an art class, we usually respond with another question. So the child gets a chance to solve problems with little help from the art teacher. This helps the child to substitute the image of the teacher as the knower. The child becomes the knower himself. He also becomes self-confident, self-reliant, innovative and creative.

*Mandu Chiloane*

Some objects surrounding us in our everyday life have been made by men and women using their creativity. To arrive at the shape of a car, a house, a bicycle or a bridge, the designer should think about how the object will look, work and be used by the society. Well-designed objects should be both functional and good-looking. To design such objects, people need to understand the elements of art like line, shape, composition, space and so on. Art teaches children the skills of creative thinking and design. They may become the designers of tomorrow. Also, art encourages children to be aware of objects, their meaning and their use.

*Nhlanhla Xaba*

Children in art classes work closely together as a group. They learn that all artworks are unique and should not be compared. They learn to be non-competitive, unlike in other subjects where they compete for marks. They show appreciation of each other's artworks by giving advice and honestly pointing out the strong and weaker parts of the works. In this way, they learn to accept criticism and develop a feeling of trust within themselves. They learn more about others' traditions and beliefs through the ideas expressed in their artworks. This makes them understand and respect each other and feel strong in their own identity. All these qualities apply in life where children are exposed to many people with different attitudes. Through art, children learn to adapt themselves to different situations and they are confident.

*Nothemba Maqalekane*

God created everyone with special inborn senses of touch, sight, smell, hearing and taste. It is through the development of these senses that we can communicate with our environment and the community. All children are naturally active and eager to explore their environment using all their senses. Young children want to touch, eat and smell all objects that they see around them – this is how they learn about the world around them. In art we encourage children to use all their senses and they are actively involved. What they experience through the senses reaches their inner soul. It is the depth of this experience that arouses creativity because every impression needs an expression.

*Thandi Dayel*

Many children are wanting more and more to fill their lives with the things that money can buy. They hope to be rich so that they can have everything that they want. Often children in the cities have little religion in their family, they have very little traditional culture and no longer live near nature. Because of these things, some children become "estranged" – this means that they feel that there is very little that they belong to and they cannot find fulfilment. Some parents do not even understand their children any more. Making and appreciating art enriches children's lives. Art allows children to feel and express their responses to the world. They learn to appreciate and love their environment, to look at the beauty in the city and in nature. They learn to involve themselves more with the things around them and not to wish for more that money buys. Art helps to develop creativity. It teaches children to find new ways of making things. For example, using waste materials, a child can see that any substance can be transformed and made into something beautiful.

*Helen Sebidi*

The human brain is divided into two parts called the left and right hemispheres. Each hemisphere stores different functions. Unfortunately in our education system only the left hemisphere is nourished and nurtured well. The left hemisphere stores logic and reason and is developed through mathematics, physics, biology, geography and language. The right hemisphere stores spontaneous and intuitive powers. This hemisphere houses our emotions and our imagination and helps us to fantasize and think creatively. It also helps us to see problems as a whole, to understand images and spatial relationships. In art children develop right brain qualities. They express their feelings spontaneously through images, they learn to see artworks as a whole and to understand spaces between and around things, they explore their imaginations and develop creative thinking. I regard the powers of the right hemisphere as important and a must for the healthy development of every human being.

*Tanki Mokhele*

Traditionally, art has always been an integral part of community life in Africa. People make masks and sculptures to use in religious ceremonies and rituals, women paint murals on the walls of their homes. Functional objects, clothing and jewellery are handcrafted. Traditional African art has an important social function and people understand the meaning of art in their lives. But in our capitalist society, art has become a commercial commodity. Artworks are displayed in galleries, seen by few people and understood by even fewer. Art has become the property of the wealthy and is inaccessible to the majority of people. Many people see artists as strange people with a mysterious talent and most people are out of touch with their own creativity. Art has become alienated from society. The neglect of art education in most schools reinforces this alienation, and many children grow up believing that art is not important in society. But art is an important part of a people's culture and it must become part of our lives again. Through art, we express our feelings and ideas about who we are and about the society in which we live. I believe that all people are essentially creative and that we need ongoing meaningful art education for everyone to realise their own creativity and to demystify art in society.

*Lindy Solomon*

Teaching art is not necessarily about training future artists. It is about teaching children to use their minds creatively and to develop awareness. Art is a way for children to explore their social relationships, understand their experiences and communicate with non-verbal symbols. Art also contributes to our society because it provides a foundation for some careers in the world of industrial art. For instance, fashion design, layout and graphic design and advertising all need visual awareness as a basis.

*Wandile Mlangeni*

After a long flight of a butterfly searching for bright and attractive colours, at last it finds a flower to rest on. I see myself like the butterfly. This is the time to bring the bright light of art to our children. Now this is the time to come together with our children and the community with all our senses and feelings. For a long time, adult artists have been working separately from children. Adults now must stand up and welcome all children into the world of art. Children and adults can become friends in art classes. Through art, children learn to observe and preserve their environment and nature. They become aware of all around them and come to understand their environment. They express their feelings and communicate with others. They feel free among the people.

*Dumisani Khumalo*

15

# Working with children

*We have thought long and hard about the values and attitudes we would like to develop in ourselves and in the children. We have also debated the kind of approach and method we should use in our teaching. After lengthy discussions, we have chosen the following principles to guide us when working with children:*

## Freedom based on discipline

When children feel free to explore, to question and to express themselves, they are most likely to learn and enjoy learning. But children can only feel free when they know what kind of behaviour is acceptable in the group – they need to know that there are limits and what these are. Discipline problems are less likely to occur if limits are made clear from the start and if activities are meaningful and well-structured. This encourages self-discipline in children. If discipline problems do occur, the teacher should consider whether the project was structured, focused and meaningful enough for the children.

## Respectfulness

Children need to experience both giving and receiving respect. If a child feels respected by the teacher and by the other children, s/he will, in turn, respect others. Similarly, if the child is listened to and acknowledged at all times, s/he will listen to and acknowledge others. Non-racial and non-sexist behaviour should be encouraged at all times. Children need to respect themselves, each other, their work and their environment. Nobody should dominate, distract or interrupt anyone else. Nobody should damage anybody else's work.

## Democracy

Everybody in the group is equally important, nobody should dominate. The teacher should not be authoritarian but should be like a guide who helps children to discover and use their own inner knowledge. With such a teacher, children will feel free to participate and express themselves spontaneously and honestly.

## Collective activity

Children should come to understand that they are individuals who are part of a group. Every child must feel that s/he belongs to the group. They should work together, sharing ideas and materials. Group projects encourage children to work collectively.

## Non-competitiveness

Children need to understand that each person is different and everybody's work is unique. There should be no comparisons between children or between their works. The learning environment should in no way encourage competiteveness. For example, if work is displayed, every child's work must be included. Discussion with children about their work is more important than marks, stars or rewards.

## Non-violence

Nobody should hurt any person, animal or plant or damage things in the environment. The teacher should never use corporal punishment (beating or thrashing). When it becomes necessary to discipline children, rather discuss *why* their behaviour is unacceptable. Then it is important to redirect their energy and remotivate them into the activity.

Two boys making clay pots, Dube.

## Self-responsibility

Children need to develop self-reliance – to take responsibility for themselves, to be independent and resourceful. They need to know how to use and care for materials and equipment, to remember to do homework tasks, to make their own decisions in their artworks and to contribute actively in group activities. They should produce work that *they* feel satisfied with rather than only to please the teacher.

## An ordered environment

Children respond well to a sense of order if they feel that they are part of it. They need a well-organised working space and they like to share the responsibility for organising materials and equipment. It is important that they also take responsibility for cleaning up – they enjoy each having their own tasks. Cleaning up can be made into an enjoyable activity.

## Active learning and participation

Education is not what the teacher gives but rather what the children experience. Children learn when they are actively involved in doing, thinking and discovering. They learn more this way than by only listening to words. Teachers need to encourage all children to participate fully in discussions and activities.

## Meaningful content

Children learn best when projects are directly related to their own experiences, needs and interests. Teachers need to talk a lot with children to arrive at meaningful content together.

Me and my dog. Pencil. Age 6. Katlehong.

## Creative thinking not imitation

Children need to learn *how* to think and not *what* to think. Teachers should never set projects which rely on imitation and copying should be discouraged at all times. Also, children should not do projects which are like recipes that they follow step by step without any creative thinking. All projects should develop creative thinking in children.

## Positive encouragement

Children develop confidence when they receive positive encouragement and constructive criticism. Negative criticism discourages and inhibits them and sometimes makes them fearful. This can have a lasting negative effect.

## Parental involvement

Education is not something that happens at certain times in special classes – it is an ongoing experience. Parents are also teachers of their children. When parents and teachers communicate regularly they can enrich each other's understanding of their children. Children enjoy sharing their learning experiences and they need their parents' active interest and positive encouragement. We encourage parents to involve themselves in their children's art activities, wherever possible. They can do this by attending parents' meetings, making contributions, collecting waste materials, helping to find venues and to fund-raise. When parents are supportive and involved in their children's education, children are more motivated and committed to learning.

# Opening the doors of creativity

Creativity is a power, an energy within each of us. With this energy, we can express our feelings, our experiences and our understanding of life. Young children express their creativity spontaneously but as they grow older, many children stop expressing themselves freely and their creative growth is stunted. Creativity needs to be nourished and developed from a young age so that it continues to grow.

Teaching children art is about encouraging them to discover and develop the creativity within them. It is about helping children use their creative energies to express themselves and their ideas freely. As art teachers, we can do this by creating a stimulating learning environment and by motivating and guiding children in well-structured art activities.

Art is an expression of life. Art classes must give children the opportunity to express their experiences of life and their responses to their environment, as well the chance to explore their imagination. An art programme for children must centre around their needs and interests. So, as art teachers, we must get to know and understand our groups of children.

## Getting to know our children

We try to find out the following information about the children in our groups:

■ What are the ages of the children? Do they fall into any of the following age groups: (5 – 7 years), (8 – 11 years) or (12 & 13 years)? If so, what are the general characteristics of this age group? Or, is it a mixed age group?

■ Where do they live? Where were they born?

■ What is their home background? What work do their parents do? What are their family's religious beliefs? What is their home language?

■ What are their emotional needs? What makes them happy? sad? worried? angry? fearful? hopeful?

■ Which school do they attend? Which subjects do they enjoy? Which subjects do they dislike?

■ How and where do they spend their free time? What are their interests and hobbies? What games do they play? Which songs do they sing? Which books do they read? What toys do they play with? Who are their friends?

■ Have they done art before? Where? What did they make? Do they make images or constructions at home and with friends?

■ Do they know about any local art forms in their area? Do they know any local artists?

As we get to know the children, we are able to answer more and more of these questions and many others. We gather this information in various ways – by asking children, chatting to parents, listening to children's discussions, watching them play, and sometimes by making contact with their teachers. Books on child psychology and children's development in art give us insight into the kinds of behaviour, needs and interests of different age groups.

When we have assessed the specific needs, likes and dislikes of the children in our groups, we can begin to structure a meaningful art programme for them.

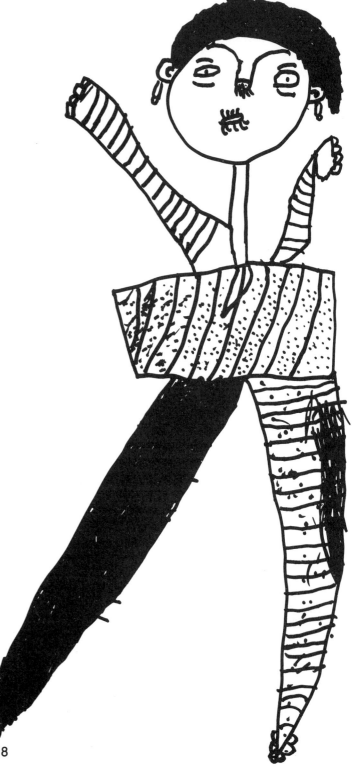

A woman. Koki pen.
Age 6. Orlando.

# Choosing meaningful subject matter

When we speak about the subject matter of an artwork, we are referring to what the artwork is about e.g. a painting of my street or a wire sculpture of a car.

Meaningful subject matter is directly related to the experiences, needs and interests of the children making the artworks. Children know best what interests them so we often discuss with *them* what themes and subject matter they would like to explore. These discussions and our growing understanding of the children help us to choose meaningful subject matter for our art classes.

In most of our art classes, we focus on *one* theme for the *whole* group to explore, rather than each child choosing their own theme. We use this approach so that we can motivate the whole group together and share ideas about the theme. Each child in the group explores the same theme differently and so children can learn from each other's exploration. For example, when exploring the theme "My street", one child may depict neighbours talking over a fence, another child may draw children playing mgusha on the side of the road, somebody else may show a funeral taking place and someone may choose to focus on casspirs and soldiers.

We discourage unfocused classes where children draw whatever they like because without some focus or direction, they tend to reproduce many of the images that they see in comics, TV, cartoons etc. We want to prevent children from repeating stereotypes again and again. We want them to create their *own* images around a theme, using good observation and their own imagination.

Sometimes a child comes to class with a particular idea or feeling that s/he wants to express – perhaps after an important experience. We then encourage this child to express what s/he wants to because the child is clearly self-motivated and needs to release this experience. However, this does not happen often and most children need a focus to work.

We are aware that there is a danger when all children work around one theme. The danger is that children might produce very similar works. To prevent this from happening, we encourage children to draw on their own personal responses and experiences and we explore many possible ways to interpret the theme.

## Some themes which we explore

*In our context i.e. urban townships on the Witwatersrand, we find the following topics and themes suitable for most of our groups.*

**Myself** – self-portrait, my feelings, me doing ordinary daily activities e.g. waking up, washing, getting dressed, eating, playing, cleaning the house, preparing for school, me playing a musical instrument, me dancing.

**My family** – granny, grandfather, mother, father, brothers, sisters.

**My friends** – portraits of each other.

**My environment** – my home, my yard, my neighbours, my street, my community, my school, the crèche, the clinic, the hospital, the church, food sellers, cafes, supermarkets.

**People at work** – digging, building, mining, farming, sewing, washing, fetching water, stamping mealies, nursing, mechanics, hawkers, coal sellers, parents at work.

**My teacher** – school teacher or art teacher.

**The games we play** – dibeke, mgusha (goomy), scotch, marbles.

**Toys and musical instruments** – wire cars, dolls, flutes, drums.

**The park**

**The city** – buildings, shopping in town.

**The rural areas** – villages, fetching water, herding cattle.

**Factories** – machines, workers.

**Outings** – the zoo, the Rand Show, the Lion Park, the circus, the aquarium, the cinema, camping and picnics in nature.

**Events** – birthdays, weddings, funerals, festivals, celebrations, stokvels, societies, music concerts, traditional dancing, school boycotts, protest marches, rent evictions.

**Transport** – the taxi rank, the bus terminus, school bus, cars, the station, trains, aeroplanes.

**Sport** – soccer, netball, swimming, running, cricket.

**Animals** – dogs, cats, chickens, cocks, hens, goats, sheep, cattle, horses and wild animals and fantasy creatures.

**Nature** – trees, plants, stones, sticks, leaves, flowers etc., landscapes, the seasons, night, day, rain, thunderstorms, sun, rainbow, fire, water, wind.

**Objects** – articles of clothing, shoes, personal objects, bicycles, masks, pots, sculptures, fruit, calabashes, cloths.

**Dreams**

**Visions of the future**

**Abstract designs and patterns**

**Stories**

Remember though, that these topics are not suitable in all contexts. It is important to focus on themes that all the children in the group have experienced in some way. For example, it is unsuitable to focus on "The Zoo" if most of the children in the group have never been to the zoo. It is also important to adapt themes for different age groups.

Hanging washing.
Koki pen. Age 6. Orlando.

# Motivating children to create

We need to encourage children to fully explore the theme or subject matter before they begin their artworks. They must feel inspired to create exciting new images. As art teachers, we have to use our own creativity to plan a meaningful experience which will motivate the children to create. Our own enthusiasm and everybody's *total* involvement in the motivation is essential.

We always motivate children at the beginning of the session. This is also the time when we give them clear focus, direction and structure to work within. We feel that motivating the children is the most important part of the art lesson. Good motivation helps to prevent children from making stereotyped images.

There are many ways to motivate children depending on the context, available resources, the subject matter or theme for the project and the age of the children.

Many of us share our venues with many other groups in the community. We move in, we teach for two hours and then we move ourselves, our work and all our equipment out again. So we do not have artrooms where we can store collections of interesting objects or display pictures and artworks on the walls. Neither do we have the space or funds to collect and store a range of useful books, slides, films, videos, tape recordings, artworks, crafts, microscopes, colour-machines or prisms! Most of us use public transport to and from the teaching venues and we often have to carry unfinished artworks and art materials with us. This makes it difficult to carry motivational resources unless these are small and light. Also, it is not often possible to take children on outings for inspiration. Working within these limitations means that we are unable to use most of the motivational resources suggested in many child art books.

In our context, we find the following methods of motivation useful and exciting:

## Looking and seeing in new ways

Artmaking is very much about *seeing*. We teach children new ways of looking at the world around them so that they begin to *see* things as if for the first time. We encourage them to look in many different ways: to look at things from far, to see things as a whole, to notice the different parts which make up the whole, to observe things from as many angles as possible, to look from above, from all sides and from below, to look inside things, to look at the spaces between and around shapes, to look at things closely, to examine minute details – the textures, the shapes, the colour changes and patterns.

For example, when we want children to look at a tree in new ways, we guide them as follows:

> Look at the tree from far away. Walk around the tree and see it from all sides.

Lie under the tree and look up at it. Can you see the branches? Look at the spaces between the branches. What shapes do you see? Look up through the mass of leaves. Can you see sunlight or sky through and in between the leaves? Do the leaves change colour when you look from different angles?

Look at the base of the tree. Can you see any roots?

Look closely at the tree to notice details. Is the bark smooth or rough? Does the colour of the trunk change? Are there any seedpods, buds or flowers? Are the leaves round, oval or fern-like?

Examine minute details. What is the pattern of the veins on the leaves? Are there worms or ants on the bark?

And so on ...

Looking at things, animals or people in this way develops our understanding of them and enriches our artworks with interesting shapes, textures, colours and details. We do lots of drawing based on detailed observation to develop our way of seeing things.

## Using all our senses for total exploration

We encourage children to explore things not only with their eyes but with all their other senses, if possible. They can explore through touching, smelling, hearing and tasting. It is best for them to close their eyes when using these senses so that they really feel the textures, hear the sounds, smell and taste fully. They can enrich their understanding of something by exploring it with all their senses.

To enrich their exploration of the tree, children can hug the tree trunk and feel the rough texture of the bark. They can climb the tree, feel the branches underfoot and the smoothness of the leaves. They can lie on the ground and feel the bumpy roots under their tummies. They can smell the leaves and sweet flowers and the earthy smell of the roots and pick pieces of bark off the tree to smell the inside of the trunk. They can even taste the bitter juice of the leaves or lick the bark and they can listen to the soft sounds of the leaves rustling in the wind.

This is a real exploration! Their drawings will be more exciting and show the richness of this experience.

A teacher motivating children to use all their senses, Orlando. The drawing on the opposite page was made by a 6 year old child after this motivation.

## Using our memories to recreate situations

Children often want to depict daily experiences (e.g. on the school bus) or events from the past (e.g. my birthday). They also like to draw or paint people who are not present (e.g. my granny). They need to remember and recreate feelings, impressions and details before they begin their artworks.

Children are very good at remembering but we need to stimulate their memories with lots of questions. We ask them about feelings, colours, shapes, textures, smells, sounds and other details.

Sometimes we help the children to re-live events through miming or acting. Children find it easy to imagine themselves in other places doing other things. Acting helps them to create images in their minds which they can use in their artworks.

For example, we could recreate the experience of "getting dressed for school" with a group of young children. Each child finds a space to work in and mimes the actions of getting dressed for school, using careful, clear and detailed movements. While they are miming, we stimulate them to remember details by asking questions:

> What do you put on first? Where do you keep your jersey, shirt, pants, socks, skirt, shoes? Are your shoes under your bed? Look for them. Do you have to undo a buckle or tie up laces? Show us how you put your shoes on.

We ask many more questions of this kind.

Before the children start drawing this activity, we also stimulate visual details with lots of questions:

> What colour is your shirt? Is it plain, striped or patterned? What is the texture of your jersey – is it woolly or bumpy? Are there any buttons or zips? Are you getting dressed in the bedroom or the sitting room? What furniture is in the room?...

Once children begin their artworks, they may need to refer to shapes and things around them for visual details that they need in their pictures. They might even need someone to model for them in different positions.

## Using our bodies to experience action

Using movement with children is a powerful way of motivating them. They love action of any kind and often have lots of extra energy to release! We sometimes begin a session with drama, miming, dancing, movement or playing games. Everybody moves at the same time, focusing on the experience rather than watching each other perform. Immediately afterwards, children create artworks to express this experience.

For example, we could begin by dividing into groups. Each group plays a game of their choice e.g. dibeke, mgusha (goomy), scotch, marbles or a ball game. Each group then makes a joint painting (on a big piece of paper) of themselves playing the game.

Children get easily overexcited and so we limit motivation through movement to five or ten minutes.

When children are motivated through action, their artworks are alive, expressive, full of movement and feeling!

## Using games to explore themes or elements of art

Children love playing games and they learn easily through game-playing. We design simple and playful activities to explore the elements of art e.g. blindfold games to explore textures, shape and space. We also use games to explore themes e.g. the "exquisite corpse" game to explore fantasy animals. In this game, we sit in a circle. We each draw the head of any animal at the top of a piece of paper. Then we fold the paper over so that no-one can see the drawing and pass it to the next person. The next person draws the body of any animal, folds over the paper and passes it on. The next person then draws the legs. Then everybody opens out the drawings to see strange fantasy creatures! It is interesting to translate these drawings into paintings or papier mâché constructions.

22

Children acting out a story wearing the masks that they have made, Diepkloof.

## Translating music and sound into art

Using sound to motivate artworks can be quite difficult but it is very exciting. We have used music and sound in the following ways.

The children each find their own space, inside or outside. They close their eyes and listen to all the sounds that they can hear – nearby and far away, loud and soft, familiar and strange. Then the whole group discusses the sounds they heard e.g. cars, a taxi hooting, the wind, a dog barking, a hen clucking, children shouting. These things become the subject matter for artworks.

We bring musical instruments or any objects which make interesting sounds to class for children to play. Then children express the experience of making music in artworks.

We encourage children to make their own sounds by clapping their hands, slapping their legs, stamping, whistling, clicking, humming etc. Children can make sounds around a theme e.g. "My street", and then make artworks based on the theme.

We sometimes select a piece of recorded music that has a strong mood. We play this a few times to the group and they listen with their eyes closed. While they are listening, they imagine an environment or an event associated with this music. Then they make free paintings based on the music.

## Storytelling

Children love listening to and telling stories. Sometimes we find a good poem or story to read or tell to the group. Or we show the children an interesting picture and encourage them to make up stories about the picture. Sometimes the children tell their own stories or stories that granny told them. Occasionally, we begin the class by singing a song and then we discuss the story in the song.

Children love chain stories. To make a chain story, we sit in a circle, someone begins a story and suddenly stops. The next person continues with their own ideas and again stops suddenly. The next person continues and so on.... until there is a complete story.

After motivating with storytelling, children make artworks using images from the stories. When there is enough time, we dramatise the story before making drawings or paintings about it. We can also make puppets or masks of characters in a story and then use them in a puppet show or play.

## Using our imagination – the power of visualising

Children are naturally imaginative and they are able to fantasize easily. We sometimes talk them through a fantasy experience, asking questions to stimulate the senses and visual details. They find it easier to concentrate with their eyes closed. We usually begin with deep breathing exercises so that they can let go of any thoughts and enter their imagination.

For example, we get children to lie on their backs with their eyes closed and we talk them through the fantasy of flying:

Take a deep breath. Listen to your breathing – in and out, in and out. Imagine now that you are lying somewhere in nature. Feel the ground underneath you. Is it grassy? Is it sandy? Is the air against your skin hot or cold? You are feeling very relaxed. Feel your body pressing heavily onto the ground. Feel it get heavier and heavier. Now feel it get lighter and lighter and even lighter. Your body feels as light as a feather resting on the ground. Now you are lifting off the ground, floating just above it, lifting higher and higher into the air. You are flying now! Are you flying on your own? Are you on a magic carpet or in a hot air balloon? Do you have wings? Do you have a wonderful flying machine of your own design? You can go as high as you like. Are you above the buildings, the trees and the clouds? Look down, what do you see? You can even fly into outer space to the stars! ...

Immediately after this, the children begin their drawings or paintings around the theme "Me in flight".

## Exploring materials

Materials themselves can be a source of inspiration. When children work with certain materials for the first time, we encourage them to experiment and explore the materials freely, in as many ways as possible. For example, we can explore the many different ways of using powder paint: thinly, thickly, watery, mixed with glue, mixed with sand, flicked, dripped, blown, splattered, scratched through etc.

## Using photographs for reference

We only use photographs to motivate children when we are not able to see the subject in our immediate environment. We use photographs from books, magazines, newspapers or calendars to look at visual details. For example, if we are exploring the theme of wild animals in Africa, we collect pictures of elephants, lions, kudu etc. We focus our discussion around the photographs, asking the children what they know about the animals and questioning them about the details that they see in the pictures. We sometimes ask them to make the sounds of the animals or to imitate their movements – this makes the theme come alive.

At all times, we make sure that children do not copy the photographs or pictures and that they use them only as inspiration for their own images and ideas. To prevent children from copying directly, we sometimes take photographs or pictures away after they have looked at them. We also encourage children to use their own compositions and backgrounds.

## Using traditional and contemporary artworks as inspiration

Sometimes we use artworks or pictures of artworks to motivate children. We discuss the artworks in detail. We talk about the artist, the materials used and why, when and where the artwork was made. Then we do practical projects inspired by the discussion and the images. For example, we might look at pictures of African masks and talk about how, when and why they were made and used. Then we make our own masks, using waste materials. In this way, we introduce children to historical and contemporary art without giving any formal lessons about history of art.

We feel that young children should begin to learn about the art made in their community, in their own country and on the continent where they live. In this way, they can begin to understand and identify with traditional culture and with artforms around them. At a later stage, they can look at art made all over the world.

So, we focus on art made in Africa, especially in southern Africa. We look at traditional artforms such as mural-painting, pottery, basketwork, cloth design, beadwork, masks, sculpture, puppets, musical instruments, body-painting etc.

We sometimes look at the artworks of well-known artists in southern Africa and, when possible, we visit artists living in our own areas to see their work and talk to them.

Occasionally, some of us take our children to art galleries to see artworks. This direct contact is best but not often possible. Mostly we have to use pictures of artworks. Books are not always available, so we collect postcards, pictures from magazines and prints on invitation cards from galleries or from printing studios. When we cannot find any photographs, we do paintings or drawings of the artworks ourselves to show the children.

Children doing a traditional firing of their claywork, Katlehong.

Children in traditional dress dancing around a fire as is done after a traditional firing, Katlehong.

All these methods of motivation are most successful when we involve the children in active discussion. We ask many questions to encourage children to be aware of details and to reflect on experiences carefully. We encourage every child to participate in discussions, even the shyest children.

We try not to rush the motivation session. We wait until the idea has ignited and everyone is excited before we start working. We prepare the materials before the motivation so that children can begin working as soon as they are inspired. They might lose their inspiration if they have to wait for materials to be organised.

If we are using materials or a technique for the first time, we demonstrate and explain carefully during the motivation session. We also give necessary guidelines at this stage. For example, if children are drawing portraits, we might encourage them to draw big and fill the page.

Motivating the children at the beginning of the session is sometimes not enough, especially with younger children. As children work, they may lose concentration or interest. If this happens, they need to be remotivated into the project. We do this by moving around and giving encouragement to those who need it. We always try to answer children's questions with more questions, to re-motivate and stimulate details. In this way, children learn to take full responsibility for their own creations and they do not rely on us for suggestions. We **never** work on a child's picture – we rather find a scrap of paper to demonstrate on, if at all. We avoid **telling** children exactly which colours to use or which details to add. Sometimes it is necessary to give a few suggestions but we always encourage them to make their own choices. If there are common problems, we give re-direction to the whole group.

Many young children seek quite a lot of attention and support while they work but older children feel quite tense when the teacher is too attentive or dominating. With all age groups, we try to prevent children from depending on us. We try not to over-motivate. We leave children to work independently for periods of time but we constantly observe and make sure that we are available and approachable at all times. We also see that there is a busy, happy and active atmosphere and that everybody is concentrating and working together.

# Learning the language of art

Children need to understand the language of art so that they can express and communicate their ideas clearly. They need to discover and explore the basic elements of artmaking: line, tone, texture, shape, colour, space and composition. We aim to give children a foundation in art by developing their awareness of these elements. We feel strongly that this should happen in the process of practical artmaking and *not* through formal academic lessons and note-taking.

We do exercises and projects especially designed to explore certain elements fully e.g. we might explore texture through a collage project. In all projects that we do, in drawings, paintings, collages, prints or sculptures, we encourage children to be aware of the elements of art as they work. We also make a point of introducing children to the vocabulary of art, by explaining the meaning of the words and using them often. When children have completed their artworks, we discuss their works as a group. This is a good time for children to talk about the elements of art in their own work.

We aim to make children aware of the following elements of artmaking at different stages of their development.

## Line

- Lines have various qualities. They can be dark, light, bold, thick, thin, long, rhythmic, fragile, curved, spidery, broken, wavy, jagged, sensitive etc.
- Lines can express feelings. We can make angry, calm, joyful, aggressive, energetic lines.
- We can change the pressure with which we draw and the way we hold the pencil (pen, stick, brush etc.) to create lines of different quality. Also, our feeling for the subject will affect the lines we make.
- Lines define shapes and forms.
- In art, lines are sometimes called *contours*.
- They appear inside forms as well as around the edges of forms.
- *Lines are alive!*

Lines with different qualities.

Lines around the edges of a form.

Lines inside and around a form.

## Tone

- Tone refers to *light and shade.*
- Forms do not have outlines in reality. They are defined by light – without light we see no forms. When drawing with tone, we have to observe very closely at how light falls on the form creating shadows in certain places. When we use tonal shading, we give forms a sense of three-dimensionality.
- Between black and white there are an infinite number of tones – *shades of grey.*
- Tonal changes can be called *values.*
- Colours also have tones e.g. we can make a range of reds from very light red (pink) to deep blood red.
- *Tonal contrast* refers to the difference between tones. The strongest tonal contrast is the contrast between black and white. A picture with strong tonal contrast is often exciting to look at.
- *A highlight* is a patch of direct intense light.
- Tone helps to create atmosphere and mood in a picture.

A drawing using only tone.

A tonal gradation chart.

# Texture

- Texture refers to the *surface feeling* of an object.
- Some textures are bumpy, rough, smooth, hard, soft, slippery, fluffy, hairy, cracked, silky etc.
- We discover texture through our *sense of touch*.
- In art, surfaces can have actual textures e.g. when we make a collage or use thick paint mixed with sand or when we create a rough surface in a sculpture.
- We can also create the illusion of texture by the way we use our materials. For example, a part of a painting can look rough from far away but when we feel it, it is actually flat.

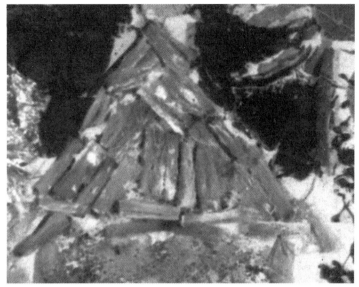

Different textures in a collage made from natural materials.

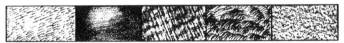

Textures drawn with a pencil.

---

# Shape

- There is an infinite variety of shapes in our world. Children should be aware of this vast range of shapes by observing the human form, animals, nature, man-made objects and buildings very closely.
- Shapes can be geometric or organic, big or small, complex or simple, angular or curvy, symmetrical or asymmetrical, textured or smooth, solid or light, transparent or opaque, clear or unclear, still or moving, separate or overlapping, flat or three-dimensional.
- Pictures and sculptures which have a variety of shapes are usually more interesting.
- Shapes which seem to have a feeling of three dimensions or which actually are three-dimensional (e.g. a construction) are often called *forms*.
- The shapes of things are sometimes called the *positive spaces* in a picture. The areas around and between the shapes are called *negative spaces*. When positive spaces are varied in size and shape, the negative spaces become more interesting. It is important to be aware of the negative spaces at all times, in two-dimensional and three-dimensional works.

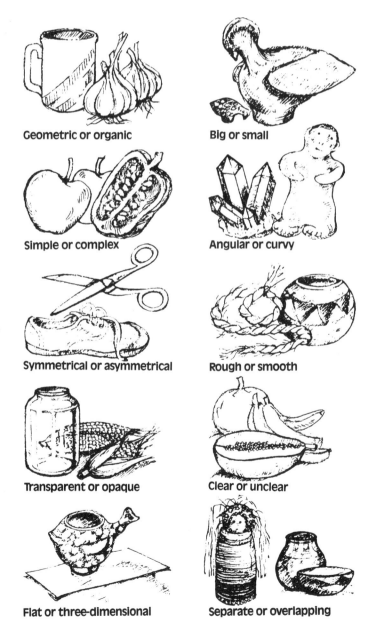

Geometric or organic

Big or small

Simple or complex

Angular or curvy

Symmetrical or asymmetrical

Rough or smooth

Transparent or opaque

Clear or unclear

Flat or three-dimensional

Separate or overlapping

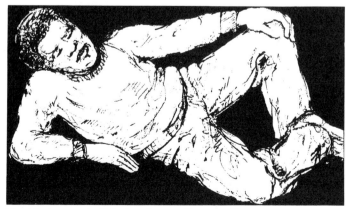

The black areas in this drawing are the negative spaces.

27

# Colour

- Mixing colours is like magic! Millions of colours can be mixed from just red, yellow and blue in different combinations.

- It helps for the teacher to know some colour theory but it is not necessary to teach formal colour theory to children. If older children express a need for some colour theory, it may be useful for them to paint colour wheels. We review some basic colour theory below.

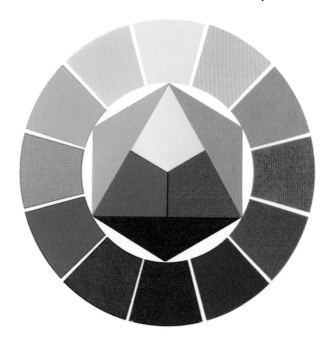

- All colours can be categorised as primary colours, secondary colours or tertiary colours:

## Primary colours:

*Red, yellow* and *blue* are the only three primary colours. They are pure colours and cannot be made by mixing other colours together. They are very intense. *All colours are made from mixing these colours in various combinations.* They lie in the centre of the colour wheel.

## Secondary colours:

These colours are each mixed with *only two primary colours.*

These lie between the primaries on the outer circle of the colour wheel.

## Tertiary colours:

These colours are mixed using *all three primary colours* together in differing amounts. Every time you mix a tertiary colour, you use red + yellow + blue.

e.g. brown = red + yellow + blue (in equal amounts)
     black = lots of blue + red + a bit of yellow.

Tertiary colours are usually *neutral,* not bright. They are often earthy browns, greys, greens, khakis, mustards, ochres, siennas etc.

- Certain pairs of colours are very strong when they are used next to each other – they provide such a strong contrast to each other that they seem to shout together. These pairs of colours are called *complementary colours:*

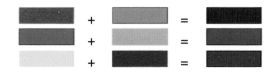

the complement of ☐ = ☐
the complement of ☐ = ☐
the complement of ☐ = ☐

Complementary colours lie directly opposite each other on the colour wheel.

Children have a natural feeling for using complementary colours, this does not have to be taught.

- If we mix a pair of complementary colours together, they *neutralize* each other:

☐ + ☐ = ☐
☐ + ☐ = ☐
☐ + ☐ = ☐

- Some colours are very similar to each other – they lie close together on the colour wheel e.g. yellow and orange. Similar colours are called *analogous colours.* When they are used near each other, they create a peaceful, harmonious effect.

- We can make light tones of a colour by adding white in different quantities. We make dark tones of a colour by adding different amounts of black. We usually mix our own black for this.

- Some colours have a feeling of heat or warmth. These are called *warm colours.* They are the colours associated with fire or sunset e.g. reds, yellows, oranges, pinks, warm browns. Some colours give off a feeling of coldness or coolness. These colours are called *cool colours* e.g. blues, greens, blue-purples, greys, peppermint-green, forest-green, icy-blue etc. Warm colours used next to cool colours create a strong contrast.

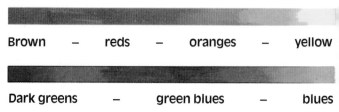

| Brown | – | reds | – | oranges | – | yellow |

| Dark greens | – | green blues | – | blues |

- There are so many millions of colours to mix and use that it is sometimes useful to limit the range for young children e.g. only primaries mixed with white or only cool colours.
- Real-life colours can be used in paintings e.g. green grass, blue sky. Colours can also be used freely when real-life colours are changed e.g. a blue face, green hair, a red tree trunk. Sometimes colour can express a feeling or a mood e.g. a face purple with anger or a blue painting to show sadness. Children often use colour freely and to express feelings. This should *never* be discouraged.
- When the same colour is used in different areas of a painting, we say that the colour has been distributed. Repeating colours in a picture is a good way of leading the eye through the painting and helps to pull it all together.

# Space and dimension

- A piece of paper is *two-dimensional* – it is flat. We can only look at a painting on a piece of paper from one side, the front.
- A sculpture or a pot is a *three-dimensional* object. It occupies space and has volume and can be seen from all sides.
- When we draw or paint, we can create a feeling of three dimensions and depth on a flat surface of paper. This effect of depth is called *perspective*. Perspective in an artwork makes some objects seem closer than others.
- There are various ways to create perspective in an artwork:

- Young children are not concerned with creating depth in their artworks. They naturally fill empty spaces with more objects and details or decorative patterns. As they grow older, they begin to discover ways of creating depth by observing their environment closely. They might need guidance but should not be taught to follow rules of perspective without observing spatial relationships in real life.

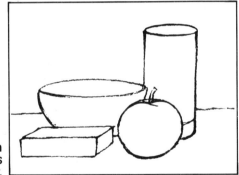

Objects which overlap others appear closer.

Closer objects are clearer, with more details and tonal contrast. Distant objects seem hazy and out of focus and do not have strong tonal contrasts.

Large objects placed lower on the page seem closer than small objects placed higher on the page.

Parallel lines seem to meet in the distance e.g. when you look down a railway line, the tracks seem to touch each other in the far distance.

Bright and warm colours seem to come towards you. Colours in the distance get duller and cooler.

29

The drawing on the right is floating in a big space.

In the drawing below, the objects are well-placed within the format. Some objects touch the edges, others are cut off by the frame. The pumpkin is the eye-catching part of the composition. This is the *focal area*.

# Composition

- Composition refers to the way that shapes are arranged in an artwork.

- In two-dimensional work, we should always see that shapes are well-placed within the format. Sometimes shapes can touch the edges, sometimes they can be cut off by the edges. Shapes should *never* float in big, empty, meaningless spaces. Children often begin by drawing small images floating on big pieces of paper, perhaps out of fear. They need to be guided to draw big, fill the page and sometimes touch the edges. It is a good idea for children to always draw a frame before beginning, so that they are aware of the edges of the composition.

- When making sculptures and constructions, we should view them from all sides and make sure that every view is interesting.

- All parts of the composition are equally important, no area should be unconsidered. Empty spaces are as important as positive shapes. There should be an interesting arrangement of positive and negative spaces. This is especially important in abstract designs and in sculptures.

- Some parts of the composition can be emphasized. These parts should be eye-catching, they should be different from the rest of the picture or sculpture e.g. an unusual colour, a different size or shape.

- The composition must be *unified*. It must pull together, it must be cohesive. This can be done with repetition. We can repeat colours, tones, shapes, textures or patterns in different parts of the artwork. When things are repeated, they create a rhythm and lead your eye through the picture or sculpture, pulling the whole thing together.

# Talking about children's artworks

When the artworks are complete, we display them on the wall or we lay them out on tables or the floor. We then discuss the artworks as a group. We begin by asking children what they liked and disliked about the project.

We encourage younger children to talk freely about what they see. They talk about what they like and dislike in the artworks and sometimes they tell stories about what is happening in their pictures or sculptures.

Older children are able to analyse their artworks in more detail. We encourage them to comment on the meaning of their works and to discuss whether they have fulfilled the aims of the project. We also discuss their use of materials and the elements of art in their work – we talk about line, tone, texture, shape, colour, space and composition.

We encourage them to talk about their own and each other's work. These discussions are open and honest and every child is given the opportunity to talk. We make sure that nobody dominates these discussions and that no comparisons are made between children. Children develop important communication skills by talking about their artworks. They also start learning how to look at and appreciate art.

# How we organise in our working conditions

We teach art under difficult conditions so we have to organise very carefully. To organise our art programmes, we begin by asking ourselves questions about our particular working conditions:

■ How long are the art lessons?

■ How many children are in the group?

■ Do the children attend regularly?

■ Is the venue used on a temporary basis and shared with other groups in the community?

■ What facilities are there? e.g. Are there tables and chairs? Is water easily available?

■ Does the venue have safe storage space for art materials?

■ Can unfinished artworks be stored at this venue while projects are in process?

■ How will works and materials be transported to and from the venue each week?

■ Can completed artworks be stored at the venue? If not, is any other storage space available? Is there any space to store three-dimensional constructions?

We see to it that we have at least two hours for each art lesson. We organise materials beforehand, we use the first 15 – 30 minutes for motivating the children and we make sure that there is enough time for cleaning up at the end of the lesson.

We have decided to work with a maximum of 25 children in a group so that each child can participate actively and receive enough attention.

We each work in different venues under different working conditions. But we all experience a few common problems, namely: irregular attendance of children, ill-equipped venues, lack of storage space and difficulties with transport.

We stress the importance of regular attendance to children and their parents. We find that when parents encourage and support their children's involvement in art, children attend more regularly. We also keep a record of each child's attendance and follow up if a child is absent too often. If children attend regularly, we can do projects which take 2, 3 or even 4 sessions to complete. We can also build on previous projects and learning experiences. In this way, children can really develop their creativity over a period of time. Art education is an ongoing process!

Playing ball. Koki pen. Age 6. Orlando.

Many of us work in venues which are not equipped for art classes e.g. dining-rooms in children's homes, private garages, community halls. Some of these venues do not even have tables and chairs but we find that children are comfortable working on the floor. We always protect all working surfaces by covering them with newspaper – this makes cleaning up easier. Since we share many of these venues with other groups in the community, our classes are sometimes disrupted and space is not always available. To solve this problem, we often work outside – children love this! When working on uneven floors or ground, we lay down sheets of thick cardboard for children to kneel and press on. This prevents underneath textures from coming through. Big flattened cardboard boxes from supermarkets are useful for this.

Most of our venues do not have safe storage space for our kits of art materials. Many of us keep our kits at our homes and carry only the necessary materials to and from the venues each week. Small school suitcases are useful for this purpose. We have to plan and organise very carefully for art lessons which require lots of materials and equipment e.g. painting, litter sculpture.

Me sweeping. Pencil. Age 5. Orlando.

Children drawing outside, Orlando.

These shared venues also do not have storage space for incomplete works in process. Unfinished artworks have to be stored elsewhere – usually at our own homes, under beds and on tops of cupboards! We therefore have to carry the works to and from venues, using public transport. It is impossible to do projects which need a long time to dry if there is nowhere to leave wet incomplete works. We always have to do projects which can be carried to and from the venue in their unfinished states. So we have to select techniques carefully to be practical e.g. glove puppets made from cloth are more suitable than those with papier mâché heads.

We also face storage problems when we want to keep completed artworks safely to exhibit for parents and the community.

On the whole, we have found that drawings, collages, paintings, prints and other flat, two-dimensional works are easy to transport and store. For this purpose, we use portfolios which we make ourselves from flattened cardboard boxes.

On the other hand, three-dimensional works like claywork, masks and wire constructions are difficult to carry and take up lots of storage space. But children love to work in three dimensions and we see this as a very important aspect of artmaking. So we try to give all children the opportunity to explore some three-dimensional techniques, even though our working conditions often make this very difficult. If we cannot transport and store the finished works, the children take their own works home. If they are still in good condition at the time of the exhibition, we display them. If not, we simply see them as important processes and forget about the products.

# Art processes and materials that we explore with children

We believe that children need to learn many ways to use art materials so that they have the technical skills to express themselves freely and to explore the various elements of art.

We expose children to a variety of art processes and techniques. They like to feel that they are learning many skills as well as having the opportunity to express themselves. Also, we find that different children respond well to different processes. Some prefer drawing while others find three-dimensional work more exciting. By exploring a variety of art processes, every child gets the opportunity to discover what s/he likes most. When children are familiar with many techniques, they are able to approach artmaking in a flexible way.

We expose children to a range of different techniques for each of the following art processes:

Drawing

Collage

Painting

Relief printing

Sculpture

Ceramics

Mask-making

Puppet-making

Most art materials are very expensive but we choose to use a basic kit of relatively cheap materials:

| | |
|---|---|
| 4B or 6B pencils | starch |
| wax crayons | wallpaper glue |
| oil pastels | cold glue |
| coloured chalks | scissors |
| coloured dyes | a cutting knife |
| tempera powder paint (red, yellow, blue, white, black) | masking tape |
| | cartridge paper |
| | clay |
| paintbrushes | lino |
| water-based printing ink | lino-cutting tools |
| rubber rollers for printing | |

We also often use waste materials, found objects and natural materials from our own environment.

We explore all these materials in as many ways as possible and use them in a variety of combinations – the possibilities are endless!

Using cheap materials and found materials helps children to realise that that they do not need lots of money to create art. With creative and flexible thinking, it is possible to transform almost anything into an exciting artwork.

Drawing a portrait in the studio. Pencil. Age 11. Diepkloof.

Portrait of a friend. Pencil. Age 13. Diepkloof.

# Drawing

Drawing is the act of making marks on a surface using line, tone and texture.

Artists draw to capture their impressions of the world around them and to express their ideas and feelings. Many artists also regard drawing as a starting point for any artwork, whether it is a painting, print or sculpture.

All young children have a natural desire to draw. They draw to express their feelings, to tell stories and to communicate their ideas to others. At the age of about two, they begin drawing scribbles on any available surface – in sand, on walls, on floors, in books, on paper and even on misty window panes with their fingers! From their scribbles, the human figure begins to emerge. With time, they begin to make their own symbols for things in their environment which are important to them e.g. the sun, houses, cars, trees and people. As they grow older, most children want to draw things in a life-like way. We encourage them to observe people and things in their environment very closely while they are drawing. In this way, they can develop the skills to draw in a life-like way.

We teach children the language of drawing by doing a variety of exercises to explore line, tone and texture. We also make sure that children observe and draw the human figure regularly. We use a variety of materials for drawing such as soft pencils, charcoal, sticks or brushes dipped in watery paint, koki pens, natural materials, wax crayons and oil pastels.

Self-portrait. Pencil. Age 8. Katlehong.

Portrait of David. Pencil. Age 11. Diepkloof.

# Drawing with line, tone and texture

*We do many exercises for children to explore line, tone and texture. You may want to read again about these important elements of drawing on pages 26 and 27. When children have done a variety of exercises, they can do sensitive and interesting drawings using line, tone and texture.*

## Exploring line

1. We do the following exercises with children for them to discover that lines have various qualities:

   ☐ Collect a wide variety of materials and tools that make different kinds of lines e.g. pencils (HB, 2B, 4B, 6B), charcoal, crayons, koki pens, ballpoint pens. You can also use sticks, feather quills, frayed pieces of rope, brushes and your fingers, all dipped into watery paint or ink.

   Encourage children to explore all these materials and to make as many different kinds of lines as they can on a big sheet of paper.

   ☐ Encourage children to scribble – this is a good way to loosen up the hand.

   ☐ Blindfold the children or tell them to shut their eyes tightly. Explain to them that they are going to take a line for a walk on a big piece of paper. Describe various ways of moving a line while they draw lines on their paper. A pencil is good for this exercise because it can make lines of many different tones and thicknesses. Talk the children through the exercise:

   Help them to imagine that they are different animals and insects leaving trails behind them: "Imagine that you are a small ant crawling across the page, now pretend you are a snail leaving a silvery trail behind you. Now you are a spider spinning a fine web, now you are a big snake slithering all over the page..."

   Ask them to feel a certain emotion and to let the feeling flow through their hands to make lines which express that feeling: "Make an angry line, a sad line, an excited line, a frustrated line, a confused line, a drunk line..."

   Encourage them to use the pencil in different ways: "Press very lightly, now push very hard, use the pencil on its side ..."

   ☐ Children can make lines while listening to music, feeling the music in their hands. They can also listen to sounds inside and outside the room and make lines for the different sounds that they hear. They can listen and hear better with their eyes closed.

   After doing these exercises, children should look carefully at the different kinds of lines that they see on their paper and describe these to each other.

**you need**

soft pencils (HB, 2B, 4B, 6B)
charcoal
wax crayons (black, white, brown)
koki pens
ballpoint pens
sticks
feather quills
brushes
watery paint or ink
cartridge paper (or similar)

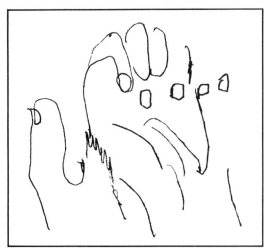

A blind contour drawing of a hand. Age 12.

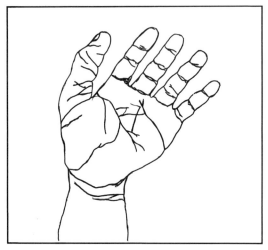

Continuous contour drawing in pencil. Age 12.

## Ideas for subject matter

Nature: trees, different kinds of sticks in an interesting arrangement, leaves with clear veins, plants, flowers, seedpods, cones, shells, birds and insects.

Buildings and outside landscapes: the yard, houses, other buildings.

Inside scenes: the kitchen, scenes through windows and doors.

Figure drawing: self-portraits using mirrors, portraits of each other, full figure drawings of models, parts of the body – hands, feet.

Objects: clothing on a hanger or crumpled showing folds, shoes, glasses, hats, baskets, wire toys, other toys, beadwork, musical instruments, masks, kites, chairs, machine parts, fruit and vegetables – whole and cut open.

Abstract designs: line patterns, cloth designs based on traditional cloths.

2. The following exercises help children to observe details very closely and to discover that lines exist both inside and around forms:

☐ **Blind contour drawing**

Draw something without ever looking at your drawing – *never* take your eyes off the subject. For example, draw your hand without ever looking at your drawing – look at your hand all the time. Sit with your head turned away from the paper, looking at your free hand so that you are not tempted to look at your drawing. Look very closely at all the lines (contours) inside and around your hand. Imagine that you are an ant crawling along all the lines – draw very slowly.

☐ **Continuous contour drawing**

Draw something without ever lifting your pencil or pen off the page. Use one continuous line – your drawing should look as if it has been made from one piece of unbroken wire. You can look at your drawing occasionally but you should keep your eyes on the subject most of the time. Study the lines inside and around the form and draw all the lines you see. For example, when you draw your hand, include fingernails, joints, wrinkles etc.

Children of 9 years and older love these two exercises. Younger children also enjoy them but they tend to cheat!

3. Children can also do *quick line drawings* while closely observing an object or a person. Time them while they do 2 minute, 4 minute and 6 minute drawings of the same subject. Emphasize that they must use only lines and no shading.

4. After all these explorations, children are ready to do *detailed line drawings*. These drawings should take a long time – 30 minutes, 1 or even 2 hours, depending on the age of the children. Remind them to use everything they have learnt about lines – to use exciting, interesting and varied lines.

Sit in this position to do a blind contour drawing of your hand.

Rural scene. Drawing with sticks and ink. Age 9. Katlehong.

Still life. Drawing with sticks and ink. Age 13. Katlehong.

Self-portrait using tone. Pencil. Age 8. Katlehong.

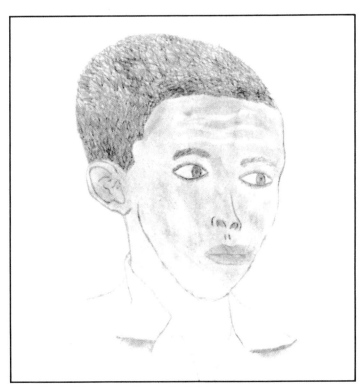

Portrait of a friend. Pencil. Age 8. Mofolo.

Portrait using line and tone. Pencil. Age 8. Orlando West.

Self-portrait. Pencil. Age 8. Orlando West.

Portrait using tone. Pencil. Age 11. Katlehong.

Portrait of Daniel. Pencil. Age 12. Diepkloof.

Portrait using line and tone. Pencil. Age 10. Katlehong.

HEBERT

Portrait using tone. Pencil. Age 13. Katlehong.

Portrait of my art teacher. Charcoal. Age 11. Katlehong.

Portrait of a friend. Charcoal. Age 11. Katlehong.

## Ideas for subject matter

**Nature:** leaves, plants, shells, seedpods, cones, stones.

**Buildings and landscapes with shadows.**

**Inside scenes with interesting lighting effects.**

**Figure drawing, faces, hands and feet.**

**Clothing:** on a person, folded or crumpled in a heap.

**Simple objects in a still life with direct lighting:** bottles, vegetables, fruit, traditional pots, bowls, glasses, teapots, cups and geometric forms – a ball, brick, box, cone.

**Imaginative drawings:** figures around a fire, landscapes with animals in moonlight, a candle-lit meal with the family, our community at daybreak, a street scene at night, the city at night, our house and yard at night, a thunderstorm with lightning.

**Tonal designs:** based on the letters of your name, based on one natural object e.g. a piece of bark.

Drawing with different pressure.

Drawing areas of lines very close together and other areas with lines spaced far apart.

Cross-hatching or criss-crossing lines.

Using a rubber to rub out some areas so that they are lighter than others.

# Exploring tone

1. We introduce children to the idea of tone by exploring light and dark in the following ways:

   ☐ We talk about the things around us which cast light e.g. the sun, electric lights, fire, lightning, the moon, stars, candles, lanterns, street lights, spotlights, torches, matches.

   ☐ If possible, we darken the room and experiment with lighted candles and torches. We look at the shadows cast on objects and on each other's faces. We move the light source around and notice how the shadows change.

   ☐ We look at shadows outside in the sunlight and observe how they change throughout the day.

   ☐ We look at deep and dark shadows e.g. when you climb in under a big, thick bush. We compare these dark shadows with lighter shadows e.g. the dappled shadow under a tree.

   ☐ We observe and discuss reflected light in water, mirrors, glass etc.

2. We use charcoal, black and white wax crayons and pencils (HB, 2B, 4B, 6B) to experiment with different tones.

3. We experiment with each of these materials on big sheets of paper, creating as many tones as possible – from very light grey through to deep black. It is easier to create tones by using these materials on their side, rather than on their tips. We create different tones by:

   ☐ drawing with different pressure

   ☐ drawing areas of lines very close together and other areas with lines spaced far apart

   ☐ cross-hatching or criss-crossing lines

   ☐ using a rubber to rub out some areas so that they are lighter than others

4. When older children have explored many different tones, they do drawings of objects using *no lines at all*. These are pure tonal drawings. We encourage them to observe the shadows and tones on the object very carefully. We tell them not to look at the lines or outlines. We encourage them to use the charcoal, crayon or pencil on its side so that they can create areas of tone to build up the object.

   Children can begin with quick tonal drawings – 2 minute, 4 minute, 6 minute drawings. Their early drawings should be done with charcoal or wax crayon, not pencil. When they find it easier to see different shades and draw with tone, they can spend more time on each tonal drawing.

Drawing of a leaf using only tone. Charcoal.

Drawing of a friend using only tone. Charcoal. Age 13. Dube.

Drawing of a friend using only tone. Charcoal. Age 12. Dube.

Still life using tone. Pencil. Age 13. Alexandra.

## Ideas for subject matter

Natural objects: bark, pieces of wood, seedpods, cacti, pinecones, feathers, fruit.

Still life arrangements of objects with different textures: shiny metallic scissors, a hairy feather duster, a prickly cactus, a smooth clay pot, a leathery shoe, a glass bottle, a beer-strainer.

Animals with interesting textures and patterns on their skins: snakes, crocodiles, lizards, whales, fish, elephants, hyenas, leopards, frogs.

Outside and inside scenes showing a variety of textures: walls, floor, windows, roofs, the ground, trees, grass.

Figures showing the textures of different parts of the body.

Abstract texture designs.

# Exploring texture

1. We introduce children to the idea of texture in the following ways:

   ☐ Children feel the different parts of their own bodies to feel the different surface textures e.g. hair, eyebrows, facial skin, lips, eyelashes, fingernails, soles of the feet etc.

   ☐ Collect many objects with interesting surface feelings e.g. pieces of tyre, a scrubbing-brush, a silky scarf, an orange, a mealie cob, sand, fur, cottonwool, sandpaper. Blindfold the children or put the objects in a packet so that the children feel these objects without looking at them.

   ☐ Children do texture rubbings of interesting surfaces in the environment e.g. gravel, bricks, floor patterns, shoe soles, leaves, bark, metal surfaces. To do a texture rubbing, lay a piece of thin paper over the surface texture. Use a soft pencil or a wax crayon to draw over the surface so that the texture comes through the paper.

   ☐ Children collect interesting surface textures e.g. sponge, cork, tyre pieces, dollies, beans, seeds, macaroni, noodles, sand etc. They all glue their textures onto one big piece of board to make a texture board. They can then also take rubbings from this.

2. When we have explored texture in these ways, we do drawings of interesting textured objects. We use line and tone to create textures e.g. prickly, shiny, smooth, or hairy. We sometimes use different materials together to show different textures e.g. pencil can create a shiny surface, wax crayon is better for rough surfaces.

Drawing of a shoe showing texture. Wax crayon. Age 13. Mofolo.

A still life with many textures.
Pencil. Age 13. Dube.

A still life with many textures.
Pencil. Age 8. Dube.

## What we have experienced exploring line, tone and texture with children

Children often ask to use pencils. They handle pencils confidently because they use them as writing tools at school. At first, they tend to use pencils faintly and to make lines which all have the same thickness. The exercises that we do to explore line, tone and texture help them to change this habit. But they need to be reminded often to use the pencil creatively.

Many children ask to use rubbers to rub out "mistakes" in their drawings. We do not allow rubbers for this purpose. We explain that there are no "mistakes" in art and encourage them to develop what they have drawn, instead of rubbing out or starting again.

We also do not allow the children to use rulers. We rather encourage them to draw freehand at all times.

Some drawing materials smudge e.g. pencils and charcoal. If we explain this to children at the beginning of the drawing session, we find that their drawings do not get as dirty.

If children are cramped and their pictures overlap each other, or if the table is too high for them, they pull the paper towards them to reach the top edge. They bend the paper over the table edge and their drawings get folded and scruffy. To avoid this problem, we encourage them to kneel on their chairs or work on the floor and we see that they each have enough space.

It is natural for young children (5 – 9 years) to draw with lines. They enjoy the line exercises and soon realise that lines can have very different qualities. They understand the difference between light and dark e.g. to show that hair is black, they press hard. After exploring tone, they become aware of different shades and they begin to use tone in a decorative way. They are not interested in using tone in a life-like way. They love the exercises to explore texture and they show an awareness of different textures in their drawings by using different line patterns e.g. spirals, stars, stripes, zig-zags etc.

Older children (10 – 13 years) are very keen to draw from close observation, using all their discoveries about line, tone and texture. They observe and draw the finest details. They do continuous contour drawing easily and they enjoy blind contour drawing, although they find this exercise scary at first. After exploring the qualities of line through various exercises, they begin to use interesting and sensitive lines in their drawings. At this age, they develop a keen interest in tone. They begin to observe shadows closely and try to create volume in their drawings. They become more skilled at creating different textures in their drawings.

My friend doing art. Pencil. Age 12. Diepkloof.

Two friends drawing. Pencil. Age 12. Diepkloof.

Children drawing a seated model, Katlehong.

# Figure drawing

*It is important for children of all ages to draw the human figure while observing a live model. Drawing the figure is not such a difficult task but children need regular practice. As they learn how to really observe the figure closely, their figure drawings improve rapidly and they develop confidence.*

1. We begin each life drawing session with some of the following exercises:

   ☐ Children explore the form of their bodies through movement e.g. they shake all the different parts of their bodies, move all their joints, pat a partner all over and mirror each other's movements. Remember not to spend more than ten minutes on movement exercises because children tend to get over-excited and distracted!

   ☐ Children do quick warm-up drawings of a model to get familiar with the shapes of the body and to loosen up their hands:
      - Blind contour drawings of the model – see page 38.
      - Continuous contour drawings of the model – see page 38.
      - 2 minute line drawings, 4 minute line drawings.
      - Gesture drawing. Scribble the figure loosely.
      - 2 minute tonal drawing, 4 minute tonal drawing.
      - Memory drawing. Look at the model for 2 – 3 minutes non-stop. When the model stops posing, draw the figure in a shadow silhouette from memory.
      - Group drawing. Each child starts a figure drawing. After 2 minutes, they all move to the next child's drawing and continue that drawing, and so on ... until the figures are complete. In this way, each drawing is made by 4 or 5 children collectively.

2. After doing some of these warm-up exercises, children are ready to do more detailed figure drawings with a model posing for a longer time. Before children start drawing, we discuss the model with them:

   What parts of the body can you see?

   What parts are hidden?

   Look at the negative spaces between the different parts of the body e.g. the space between the legs.

   Compare the sizes of the different parts of the body e.g. the size of the head compared with the rest of the body.

   Look at the details e.g. the wrinkles, folds and patterns of the clothing, buttons, belts, jewellery, pockets, zips.

3. While they are drawing, we remind them to spend more time looking at the model than at their drawing. We tell them to draw what they *see*, not what they *think* they see or how things *should* be. We encourage observation at all times and *never* use laws, rules, tricks, mathematical diagrams, stick figures, ruler measurements or rubbers. It is natural for young children to distort and exaggerate parts of the figure. Their drawings express feeling and seldom have accurate proportions. If the children are content with their figures, we do not correct them.

4. Figure drawing should be done regularly and explored with many different materials e.g. charcoal, pencil, wax crayons, paint, oil pastels. We also combine figure drawing with other techniques e.g. wax resist, crayon and multicrayon engraving, painting, collage, printing and mixed-media.

## you need

soft pencils (HB, 2B, 4B, 6B)
charcoal
wax crayons (black, white, brown)
koki pens
ballpoint pens
sticks
feather quills
brushes
watery paint or ink
cartridge paper (or similar)

Figure leaning on a table. Brush drawing with tempera powder paint. Age 13. Diepkloof.

Portrait of Ellen Kuzwayo. Pencil. Age 5. Orlando.

Two friends modelling. Pencil. Age 5. Chiawelo.

A standing figure. Pencil. Age 6. Chiawelo.

Fifteen-minute warm-up sketches of my art teacher posing in different positions. Pencil. Age 8. Dube.

Fifteen-minute warm-up sketches of my art teacher posing in different positions. Pencil. Age 13. Dube.

My art teacher modelling in a seated position. Pencil. Age 13. Dube.

## Suggestions for the model

- Use members of the class to model. One child should not model for too long – each child must do some drawing in the session. Occasionally, you may be able to get someone outside of the group to model for the class e.g. a child's mother, brother etc.

- Pose the model in the centre of a circle of students. Each child will then sketch a slightly different view of the model.

- Change the action and direction of the model with each new pose. Let the model choose different and interesting standing, sitting and lying positions.

- Sometimes use a few models at the same time for a group figure drawing.

- Dress the model in interesting clothing – a patterned jacket, a turban, jewellery, a decorative cloth, a bright shawl, etc.

- Give the model a setting – a colourful cloth behind him/her, a still life arrangement next to him/her, bright cushions to lie on, etc.

- Let the model do an activity – read a book, knit, play a musical instrument, play with a toy, etc.

- Let the model move – skip, dance, play with a ball, etc.

My teacher posing with a hosepipe.
Pencil. Age 12. Orlando.

A standing figure. Pencil. Age 10. Diepkloof.

A tonal figure drawing. Charcoal. Age 15. Dube.

# Ideas for drawing the model

■ Encourage children to draw a whole figure filling the page or to draw a part of a figure cut off by the edges of the page. They may want to include a very simple background.

■ Children can draw the model in the real environment of the venue, with windows, light fittings, floorboards etc. in the background, and maybe also with some of the other students drawing.

■ If a setting has been created around the model, children can include this in their drawings.

■ Challenge the children to use their imaginations in drawing. Encourage them to create a theme or fantasy background around the model.

■ Older children can overlap and superimpose different figure drawings in one exciting composition. For this exercise, the model needs to pose in a few different positions for about 5 minutes each.

A friend modelling in traditional Xhosa dress with a patterned cloth behind her. Koki pen. Age 14. Katlehong.

My art teacher. Pencil. Age 11. Katlehong.

My art teacher. Pencil. Age 13. Katlehong.

My art teacher. Pencil. Age 13. Katlehong.

My art teacher. Pencil. Age 13. Katlehong.

## What we have experienced doing figure drawing with children

At first, children of all ages tend to draw small figures – perhaps because they lack confidence. They need constant reminding to draw big and fill the page.

Young children (5 – 9 years) find it difficult to concentrate when observing a model but short poses are important for them to develop their body-image. It is natural, at first, for young children to draw figures with very big heads and to leave out certain parts of the body e.g. hands, feet and joints. After movement exercises and with careful observation, they begin to understand the body structure better and include more details in their figure drawings. As they grow older, finer details appear in their drawings e.g. fingernails, toes, earrings, shoelaces etc.

Older children (10 – 13 years) love figure drawing and do wonderful confident drawings based on detailed observation. They often exaggerate facial expressions, details and proportions. As they grow older, it becomes important to them to draw with life-like proportions. By the age of 13, they are usually able to draw figures with quite accurate proportions.

We find that it is easier for children to draw figures with accurate proportions when they place their paper at an angle. We do not have easels, so we use strong cardboard or masonite board to press on. The children rest a board on their laps and lean it against a table while they draw the model.

A child drawing on a board which is resting on her lap and leaning against the table.

My art teacher. Pencil. Age 14. Katlehong.

My friend leaning against some stacked tables. Koki pen. Age 13. Diepkloof.

# Drawing with natural materials

## you need

natural materials to draw with
cartridge paper (or similar)
water

### How to make a piece of charcoal

1. Put a stick in the fire. Wood from a willow tree is best for this.
2. Remove it before it burns to ashes.
3. Get rid of the glow by dipping the stick in water.
4. When it cools down, it is ready for use.
5. You can simmer the charcoal stick in melted wax for thirty minutes. This helps to bind it. Then dry it on a paper towel.

### Ideas for subject matter

Children often like to do drawings of the landscape in which they are working. We do not set subject matter for this project because children naturally create free and imaginative artworks with natural materials.

1. Work in an area where there is some nature – trees, plants and soil. A day trip into the country stimulates children's creativity. If it is not possible to organise a day trip, work in a nearby park or in any small patch of nature.

2. Encourage children to search the area for any materials which can make marks on paper e.g.

   burnt wood for black (charcoal)

   ash for grey

   bird-droppings and milky plant juices for white

   berries and clay for reds

   clay, soil, mud, pollen from flowers and powders from certain mushrooms for browns, yellows and mustards

   crushed leaves or grass for greens

   squeezed flowers for purples, blues, reds, oranges etc.

3. Children then draw with these materials. They apply the materials with their hands. Sometimes they use them as they are, sometimes they need to mix them with a bit of water and sometimes they need to crush and squeeze the juice from them.

*Age:* Children of all ages love working with natural materials.

*Time:* Children can make drawings in one session.

## What we have experienced drawing with natural materials with children

Children have a strong feeling for nature and they enjoy the freedom of drawing with natural materials. They become aware of what nature has to offer and they realise that they can make art without using commercial art materials.

In urban townships children have little chance to experience and enjoy nature. We find that organised outings into nature are always successful. Children get inspired and make beautiful artworks.

Young children get very involved in the experience of using natural materials. They work freely and do not worry about subject matter. Teachers should not be too concerned with the products but should allow children to explore the materials freely.

Children sometimes tear the paper in their enthusiasm. Warn them about this beforehand.

We tell children to collect material and then gather in *one* area to work. This makes it easier for us to supervise and remotivate, if necessary.

We warn children about poisonous plants or mushrooms in the area. We point out which plants to avoid and explain why.

We usually take a bucket with us because water is not always close at hand. Water is necessary to mix some of the natural drawing materials and also for washing hands.

Every child should wear an overall because working with natural materials is very messy.

Drawing with natural materials is an excellent way for children to explore tertiary colours.

Some natural materials smudge e.g. charcoal. To prevent smudging, we fix the drawing with hairspray or we iron the back of the drawing. These drawings must be stored carefully and separately from other artworks.

Drawing using charcoal, soil, flowers and grass. Age 7. Orlando.

Drawing using charcoal, flowers, soil and grass. Age 7. Orlando.

Orlando power station. Drawing using clay, grass and flowers. Age 13. Diepkloof.

# Drawing with wax crayons

## you need

wax crayons — lots of colours and thicknesses
cartridge paper (or similar)
newspaper

A soldier in Soweto on June 16. Wax crayons. Age 11. Orlando.

1. Encourage the children to apply the crayons with heavy pressure. This makes the colours strong and vibrant. Newspaper padding under the artwork helps.

2. Encourage children to work directly on the paper with the crayons. If children wish to do sketches first, they should use a very light coloured crayon. Do not allow children to sketch in pencil first and then "colour in" with crayons — blunt crayons are not suitable for the details of a pencil sketch. Crayons work most effectively for all age groups when used boldly and spontaneously.

3. Encourage children to work big — to fill the page and cover large areas solidly with colour. Remind them that the edges of the paper are as important as the centre. Tell them that you want to be able to see their pictures from the other side of the room!

4. Encourage children to use contrasting colours e.g. neutral colours (grey, brown) with primary colours (blue, red, yellow). Don't forget about the unusual colours such as ochre, olive green, midnight-blue.

5. The children can create their own interesting colours and tones if they apply one colour over another. We call this overlaying crayon over crayon.

6. Children can give their completed crayon works a shiny finish by rubbing them with folded tissue.

7. Encourage children to experiment and really explore different ways of using crayons e.g. overlays, scratching and engraving into their crayon works, mixing long and short strokes, thick and thin strokes, texture-rubbings. We will describe three special wax crayon techniques you can use with the children — wax resist, crayon engraving and multicrayon engraving. But encourage them to also experiment with their own techniques!

8. Wax crayons are very suitable for group projects e.g. murals on paper. Four to eight children can work on one large piece of paper using a common theme.

**Age:** All ages.

**Time:** Children can easily finish wax crayon drawings in one session. More detailed works may take longer.

## What we have experienced using wax crayons with children

Wax crayons are relatively cheap, easy to use and long-lasting. You can buy them at many shops, and some suppliers or factories are willing to donate reject and broken crayons. It is best to get a selection of thick and thin wax crayons. The thick (chubby) crayons are stronger and last longer than the thin crayons. However, the thinner crayons are available in many more colours.

We take crayons out of their boxes and put them together in a large box or tin so they can be used communally. The children can then share the more unusual colours — this saves expenses.

Younger children (5 — 7 years) respond very positively to wax crayons. They use the chubby crayons confidently and freely. Group projects with this age group are very successful.

Children from 8 to 11 years old also enjoy using wax crayons but they prefer the thinner crayons which allow for more detailed work. This age group manages overlaying crayons very well, as well as group murals in crayon.

Children of 12 years and older sometimes think that wax crayons are "boring" and that they are for younger children. However, wax crayons can be very exciting for this age group if they are encouraged to combine different techniques in one work e.g. crayon overlays, crayon engraving, multicrayon engraving, wax resist and textural exploration.

Children of all ages often use wax crayons in a light sketchy way, resulting in weak pale drawings. At the very beginning, we demonstrate how to apply the crayons with heavy pressure. We remind them regularly to press hard and to avoid weak light strokes. Many children fear breaking crayons if they press too hard. Some refuse to use broken crayons. We reassure them that a broken crayon is just as useful as an unbroken one. We let them see us using broken crayons!

Many children ask to use pencils first because they are familiar with them as writing tools. Break this habit immediately! Allow them to scribble freely with crayons on spare paper in order to build their confidence.

Young children tend to tear the edges of the paper when they apply crayon with heavy pressure. Advise them to be extra careful near the edges.

Explain very clearly what it means to cover the whole paper with colour. This is sometimes misunderstood and children suddenly scribble over complete drawings.

Children sometimes ask if they can turn over and start again. We explain that there are no mistakes in art. We encourage them to complete every work.

Remind children to pick up all crayons — broken or unbroken — off the floor. Otherwise they will trample on them and destroy them.

## Ideas for subject matter
All subjects can be explored with wax crayons — see page 19 for ideas.

A policeman threatening school children on June 16, 1976. Wax crayons. Age 11. Orlando.

My friend. Wax crayons. Age 10. Katlehong.

Me and my house. Wax crayons. Age 5. Diepkloof.

My friend. Wax crayons. Age 8. Katlehong.

My friend. Wax crayons. Age 12. Katlehong.

My teacher. Wax crayons. Age 10. Orlando.

Self-portrait. Overlayed
wax crayons. Age 11.
Katlehong.

Soldiers in the township. Wax crayons. Age 13. Dube.

wax crayons
black tempera powder paint
a little liquid soap or a small bar of soap
paintbrushes
sharp tools e.g. nails, knives, thorns, sharp
sticks
cartridge paper (or similar)
newspaper

# Crayon engraving

## How to do crayon engraving

1. Place newspaper padding under your paper to press on.

2. Using wax crayons, cover the *whole* surface of the paper with different colours. Press hard and with even pressure. Remember that no white paper must show through.

3. Later we will cover the wax crayons with black paint, so white and bright or light colours work well because they stand out strongly against the black. Do not use black crayon. Gold, silver or copper crayons are metallic and do not work well.

4. Shake any lumps or flecks of wax crayon off the paper.

5. Mix black tempera powder paint with water until it is like black milk. Add a drop of liquid soap to the paint or rub your paintbrush on a bar of soap. This helps the paint to stick to the surface of the paper without peeling off.

6. Apply a layer of black paint over *all* the wax crayon until no colours show through. The layer of black paint must not be too thick.

7. Leave your paper to dry completely.

8. Now you are ready to begin engraving your design. Use a sharp tool (e.g. a nail) to engrave through the black paint so that the colour shines through. Engrave some thick lines and some thin lines. You may even scrape away whole areas – a knife is good for this. Create different textures and patterns with different sharp tools.

*Age:* This technique is good for children of 7 years and older.

*Time:* Crayon engraving usually takes at least two sessions. The first session is for covering the paper with wax crayon and then black paint. The second session is for engraving the design. A detailed work may need another session. Because this technique takes so long, young children should not work on very large paper.

## What we have experienced doing crayon engraving with children

Children think this technique is like *magic!* They say that the bright colours come shining through the black "like twinkling stars in the night". They feel that they are scratching through "mud to find jewels"!

At first, some children are afraid to press hard with the wax crayons. We remind them that the magic doesn't work if their colours are weak.

It is wise to check each child's work before it is painted black. Check that their colours are strong and evenly applied. Children sometimes get so excited that they rush the crayon work and leave patches of paper showing through.

We always make sure that the children write their names on the back of their paper before they apply the black paint. Otherwise, when all their works are black, the children will not know which is theirs.

Children do not like to cover their bright coloured pattern with black paint. They think that they are spoiling their design. We find it useful to demonstrate the whole process at the beginning of the lesson. The children then know what to expect.

It takes care to mix and apply the black paint correctly. We recommend that the teacher mixes the black paint to the right consistency and tests the paint over some wax crayon on a separate piece of paper. We never paint directly onto children's work — they can get very upset and discouraged. If the paint is too thick, the colours will lose their brightness and become blackish. If the paint is too thin, it will be difficult to engrave through it. Also there will be little contrast between the black paint and the wax colours.

If you do not add soap to the paint, it may chip off later. Also do not leave the works to dry in direct sunlight. This can cause chipping.

Watch that the children do not engrave with too much pressure. They sometimes tear the paper.

Children are sometimes so excited by the technique that they rush their designs and forget to make interesting compositions of varied shapes, lines, textures and patterns. They are quickly satisfied with sketchy pictures and with only thin lines. We remotivate them to make interesting details and encourage them to scrape away some large areas so that lots of colour shines through. It helps if they base their designs on preliminary sketches that they have done in the previous session.

This technique is quite messy because the paint flecks fly around during the engraving process. Children must protect their clothes. Also, if the tables and floors are covered with newspaper, it is easy to clean up afterwards.

## Extra ideas for crayon engraving

- Encourage children to use different kinds of engraving tools to create different textures and lines. For example, a thorn will create a fine line and a knife can scrape away large areas.

- If you have some oil pastels, you can apply these over the black painted areas for another effect. You can engrave patterns into the pastel areas too!

- You can use black wax crayon instead of black paint.

- You may use brown paint instead of black paint. In fact, you can use any colour that contrasts strongly with the wax colours.

### Ideas for subject matter

This technique is especially suitable for subjects that have interesting designs, textures and patterns e.g. insects, flowers, leaves, brightly-designed cloths, musical instruments. Imaginary designs based on animals and birds work well. The effect created is very similar to the Shangaan embroidery on black fabric.

Night scenes in the city, township or country are very exciting in this technique.

People and houses. Crayon engraving. Age 5. Chiawelo.

A boy herding cattle. Crayon engraving. Age 9. Katlehong.

Fish. Crayon engraving. Age 7. Katlehong.

My street. Crayon engraving. Age 13. Katlehong.

Neighbours talking over the fence. Crayon engraving. Age 13. Dube.

Portrait of a man. Crayon engraving with mustard paint and oil pastel overlays. Age 13. Diepkloof.

A leaf, drum and scissors. Crayon engraving using black wax crayon instead of black paint. Age 11. Mofolo.

Self-portrait. Crayon engraving with brown paint. Age 11. Diepkloof.

wax crayons
sharp tools e.g. nails, scissor points, knives, thorns, toothpicks, sticks
cartridge paper (or similar)
newspaper

# Multicrayon engraving

## How to do multicrayon engraving

1. Place newspaper padding under your paper to press on.

2. Cover the whole page with a light coloured wax crayon e.g. yellow, light pink or grey. Press hard and with even pressure.

3. Then cover this first layer of colour with a slightly darker colour. This time do not press too hard because you do not want to break through the underneath colour.

4. Now cover this again with a darker colour. Add another layer of an even darker colour on top and so on... You can do about three, four or five layers. The last layer must be the darkest – black crayon is best.

5. Rub the surface gently with tissue to remove any flecks or lumps of crayon.

6. Now you are ready to engrave your design. With a sharp tool, engrave through the black layer. Engrave lines and scrape away areas to create textures and patterns. If you press lightly, the darker colours in the top layers will show. If you press harder, the lighter colours in the deeper layers will show. Changing the pressure on the tool allows different colours to shine through.

7. It is a good idea to limit the colour range you use e.g. only warm colours: yellow, pink, orange, red, brown and then black, or only cool colours: grey, green, blue, purple and then black.

*Age:* All ages.

*Time:* At least two sessions are needed for multicrayon engraving, one to apply the layers of colour from light to dark and another to engrave the design. Detailed works may need an extra session. Because this technique takes so long, the children should not work on very large paper.

## Extra ideas for multicrayon engraving

■ Encourage children to use different kinds of engraving tools to create different textures and lines.

■ Older children can combine this technique with crayon engraving in one work. The combination can create interesting effects.

## What we have experienced doing multicrayon engraving with children

Children of all ages find this technique very exciting and they are able to create dramatic effects.

However, it is quite a difficult technique and so we always demonstrate the whole process of layering and engraving at the beginning of the session. We also guide children carefully throughout the process.

This technique does not work unless the layers of crayon are applied strongly and with even pressure. We take time to help the children find the right pressure for the wax layering – not too hard and not too soft. If children break through underneath layers, we remind them not to press too hard.

Younger children tend to rush their layers of crayon and they often leave some areas uncovered. We remind them to cover every inch of the paper, right to the edges and we give them lots of time to do this properly.

We check each child's work often during the layering process and before they begin engraving. Sometimes children are so eager to engrave that they do not finish their crayon layering properly.

Children need to be careful not to engrave right through the paper!

Children also tend to rush their engraving. They find the technique so exciting that they forget to pay attention to their compositions, forms, lines and details. It sometimes helps if they base their designs on preliminary sketches that they have done in a previous session.

This is a very messy technique because hundreds of crayon flecks come off during the engraving. Children must protect their clothing. Also, remember to cover tables and the floor with newspaper.

## Ideas for subject matter

Themes with a strong mood or atmosphere work well. Layers of warm colours create a hot fiery mood, layers of cool colours create a sad mood or cold effect.

Landscapes in different weather conditions, with watery, fiery or earthy effects can be very dramatic in this technique.

Two figures. Multicrayon engraving. Age 13. Diepkloof.

A landscape.
Multicrayon engraving.
Age 12. Dube.

A man and a cupboard. Multicrayon engraving.
Age 5. Diepkloof.

A portrait. Multicrayon engraving. Age 5.
Diepkloof.

A figure. Multicrayon engraving. Age 11. Diepkloof.

68

Two boys.
Multicrayon engraving.
Age 13. Diepkloof.

A casspir and soldiers in Soweto. Multicrayon engraving. Age 12.
Diepkloof.

A boy making wire cars. Multicrayon engraving. Age 11. Mofolo.

# Wax resist

wax crayons
one or more colour dyes
paintbrushes
jars of clean water
cartridge paper (or similar)
newspaper

## How to do wax resist

1. Place newspaper padding under your paper to press on.

2. Do a design or drawing using wax crayons only. Press hard so that the wax will resist the dye later. White crayon is very effective for this technique. Do not cover the whole paper with solid colour – some areas of white paper must be left unwaxed.

3. When you are satisfied with your drawing or design, cover the whole paper with a thin layer of colour dye. The wax will resist the watery dye and the dye will slip off the wax. This is why we call this the wax resist technique. The bright colours will shine through the dye. You can use one colour wash only over the whole picture or you can use different colour dyes over different areas of the picture. But do not paint layer over layer – one thin dye wash is enough. Remember to paint the dye *over* the wax crayon.

*Age:* All ages.

*Time:* This technique can be done in one session. A detailed work may take two sessions.

## Extra ideas for wax resist

- You can also use the wet resist method. Before you paint over the wax drawing, wet the whole paper and the drawing with water. Then blow, drop, flick and float the dyes over the surface. This creates a watery effect.

- Sometimes it can be effective to leave some white areas of paper without wax or colour dye.

- If you do not have dyes available, you can mix tempera powder paint with water to get the consistency of dye. Make sure the paint is thin and watery.

- Watercolour paints work just as well as dyes.

### Ideas for subject matter

Because of the watery effect it creates, this technique is effective for scenes in the rain, storms and underwater scenes.

## What we have experienced doing wax resist with children

Children love this technique – they are fascinated by the way the wax crayons magically resist the dye wash!

We always demonstrate the whole technique clearly at the beginning of the session. Otherwise children refuse to paint dye over their designs. They think that all their work will be spoilt.

Children tend to apply too much dye and their works become soggy. Sometimes the resist technique does not work if there is too much dye.

If the wax crayons do not shine through the dye, then it means that the children have applied the wax crayons too lightly. Check their drawings before they apply dye.

We demonstrate clearly how to wash the paintbrush each time a new colour dye is to be used. Children must learn that if they dip a dirty brush into a clean dye, the colour will be spoilt forever. If we have enough paintbrushes, we provide a different brush for each colour dye – this prevents the children from spoiling the dyes.

It is best to have the jars of dyes in one area on newspaper. Let the children come to that area one by one to paint their dye washes. This will prevent spilling and spoiling of dyes with dirty brushes.

Remember that dyes stain! Children must protect their clothes.

The dye takes a while to dry. Put works in the sun while the children are cleaning up.

A still life on a table. Wax resist using black tempera paint wash. Age 13. Katlehong.

Trees. Wax resist using purple dye wash. Age 14. Katlehong.

A man, a dog and a child. Wax resist using black tempera paint wash. Age 10. Diepkloof.

71

# Drawing with oil pastels

*you need*

oil pastels – a range of colours
cartridge paper (or similar)
newspaper

1. Encourage children to use oil pastels boldly. They need to press quite hard to create rich, vibrant effects. Newspaper padding under the artwork helps.

2. Encourage children to work confidently and freely. If they wish to do sketches first, they should use a light pastel or a piece of chalk. They should never use pencil to sketch their designs.

3. Encourage children to cover large areas with colour. They can cover the whole surface with pastel or they can choose to leave some paper showing through in places. Either way, they should think about every area – the edges and the background too.

4. Encourage children to use contrasting colours and tones e.g. bright colours next to dull colours, light colours alongside dark colours. They can create lighter tones by applying white pastel over a colour e.g. white over red makes pink.

5. The children can create their own unusual colours if they apply colours on top of each other – pastel overlays.

6. Children can experiment with different ways of using oil pastels to create different textures e.g. boldly applied, lightly applied, overlayed, short stubby strokes packed closely together, stippled dots, long free strokes, scribbled areas, scratching and engraving, rubbing some areas with tissue.

7. Children can give their completed oil pastel works a smooth, marbly surface by rubbing them with soft tissues.

8. Oil pastels are bright and colourful and very suitable for group murals.

*Age:* Oil pastels are easy to use and therefore suitable for all ages.
*Time:* Children can complete oil pastel drawings in one session. More detailed works take longer.

## What we have experienced using oil pastels with children

Children are excited by the brightness of oil pastel colours. They enjoy them because they are soft and easy to apply over big areas. They also enjoy overlaying colours and seeing how easily they mix.

As with wax crayons, at first they tend to use the pastels in a light, sketchy way.

If oil pastels are kept loosely together in a container, they dirty each other and colours are spoilt. We always keep them in their boxes which have ridges to separate colours.

Encourage children to use broken oil pastels right to their ends!

Oil pastels do stain tables and clothes. Newspaper is essential on all surfaces and children must protect their clothing. Grubby hands are a natural outcome of using pastels – see that water and soap are available for washing after the lesson.

Remind children to pick up all pastels and pieces of pastel off the floor. It is no easy job cleaning pastel off floors! Oil pastels have an oil base and do not come off with water alone, so a soap or detergent is necessary.

## Extra ideas for using oil pastels

■ Oil pastels can be combined with wax crayons, chalks, paint, collage or dyes to create exciting mixed-media artworks.

■ Oil pastel resist is a special technique with oil pastels and paint. We explain this in detail next.

### Ideas for subject matter

All subjects can be explored with oil pastels – see page 19 for ideas.

Self-portrait. Oil pastels. Age 12. Katlehong.　　A man herding cattle. Oil pastels. Age 9. Katlehong.

My father at work. Oil pastels. Age 12. Dube.

73

The taxi rank.
Oil pastels.
Age 6.
Diepkloof.

The taxi rank.
Oil pastels.
Age 10.
Diepkloof.

The taxi rank.
Oil pastels.
Age 11.
Diepkloof.

Women from the
Methodist church.
Oil pastels.
Age 10.
Dube.

Women on their
way to church.
Oil pastels.
Age 12.
Dube.

# Oil pastel resist

oil pastels
chalk
black tempera powder paint
paintbrushes
cartridge paper (or similar)

## How to do oil pastel resist

1. Do a detailed line drawing with a piece of coloured chalk. Use a colour which is different from the colour of the paper that you are working on. Use thin and thick lines.

2. Colour in between the chalk lines with different coloured oil pastels. Do not cover the chalk lines. Some areas can be left uncovered.

3. Apply the oil pastel with heavy pressure so that it will resist the black paint later.

4. Bright and light oil pastels are very effective, especially white and grey. Do not use black oil pastel because this will not show through the black paint.

5. Mix black tempera powder paint with water until it has the consistency of black milk. Draw with some oil pastel on a sample piece of paper. Then paint over the oil pastel. The oil pastel should resist the black paint – the colours should shine through. If this does not happen, either the black paint is too thick or the oil pastel has been applied too lightly.

6. When the consistency of the paint is correct, gently apply one layer of black paint over the whole oil pastel drawing. It is best to use a soft brush to do this. The paint will slip off the oil pastel areas but it will cover the chalk lines and any areas of the paper which are not covered with oil pastel. Remember to paint only one layer otherwise the resist technique might not work.

*Age:* All ages.

*Time:* This technique must be done in one session. The black paint must be applied as soon as the oil pastel drawing is complete, otherwise the resisting oil in the pastels will dry out and the resist technique may not work.

## Extra ideas for oil pastel resist

■ You can use dyes instead of paint.
■ You can apply a coat of clear varnish over the completed work when it is totally dry. This makes the colours even more brilliant.

### Ideas for subject matter

Oil pastel resist is most effective for subjects which have bright colours, exciting patterns and designs e.g. birds, insects, animals, fantasy and imaginary themes.

## What we have experienced doing oil pastel resist with children

As with the wax resist technique, children are excited by the magical resist effect.

It is important to demonstrate the whole technique at the beginning of the session so that children understand why they need to cover their drawing with black paint.

We have found it quite easy to do this technique in one session because the initial chalk drawing and oil pastel colouring do not take very long. Children find it very easy to apply oil pastel in large areas.

Before the children paint black, check that their oil pastel drawings have a variety of colours, interesting patterns and textures and some open spaces. Also check that the oil pastel has been applied with heavy pressure.

We recommend that the teacher mixes the black paint and tests its consistency in advance. It must be ready for the children to use soon after they have finished their drawings.

Children tend to apply far too much paint. Encourage them to apply only one thin layer of paint to ensure that the resist technique works.

Self-portrait. Oil pastel resist using green and purple dye. Age 12. Dube.

The Rand Show. Wax crayons and oil pastels. A group mural made by older children (10 – 12 years). Diepkloof.

The Rand Show.
Wax crayons and oil pastels.
A group mural made by young children
(4 — 6 years). Diepkloof.

Portrait of a friend. Magazine-piece collage. Age 13. Diepkloof.

# Collage

We can make a picture or a design by sticking different kinds of papers, pieces of fabric or textured materials onto a flat surface. A picture or design made in this way is called a collage. Collage comes from a French word "coller" which means to stick and paste.

For hundreds of years, people from many cultures have made pictures using the collage method of cutting and pasting. African women use a form of collage when they sew pieces of fabric and beads in complex designs onto blankets. Also, some people cover their walls and ceilings with collages of cut-out images from magazines, especially in homes which are built from corrugated iron.

Collage elements were first used in paintings in the early twentieth century by two French artists called Picasso and Braque. Since then, collage has become a popular technique and many artists today make collages or use collage elements in their paintings or drawings.

We make collages with children using waste materials, natural materials and coloured pages from old magazines. When they make collages from found materials, children learn that they can create artworks without buying expensive art materials.

# Waste material collage

## you need

waste materials
glue
strong paper or cardboard
scissors

1. Ask children to collect waste materials at home and to pick up interesting pieces of litter outside e.g. plastic, wool, cloth, newspaper, magazine paper, toilet paper, tissue paper, aluminium foil, wrapping paper, thin rubber, serviettes, leather, old doilies, hessian, string, cotton, sweet papers, labels, paper bags, matches, sand, sandpaper, rice, noodles, old prints, used cards, pieces of torn paintings, sawdust, bus tickets, cigarette boxes, netting, orange bags, old stockings, cardboard box pieces, cottonwool and so on ...

2. Motivate children to cut out and tear interesting shapes from the waste materials they have collected.

3. Encourage children to arrange their shapes into an exciting composition on their paper. They can experiment with different arrangements and move the shapes into different positions before they glue them down.

4. Encourage children to use some big shapes and some smaller shapes for details.

5. Encourage them to overlap their shapes in some places.

6. Discuss colour contrasts and tonal contrasts. Show them how they can separate forms and make shapes clearer by placing contrasting colours and tones next to each other.

7. Encourage them to look carefully at the spaces between shapes (the negative spaces).

8. When they are satisfied with their composition, they can glue down their shapes. Every shape must be glued down firmly. Check that everything is flat.

*Age:* Children of 5 years and older.
*Time:* Waste material collages with big shapes and few details can be done in one session. More detailed works take longer.

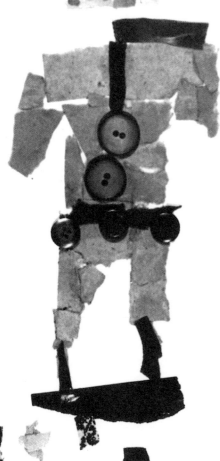

A figure made from waste paper, fabric, wool and buttons. Age 9. Orlando.

## What we have experienced making waste material collages with children

We ask children to begin collecting materials a few weeks before we do the collage project. They are quite forgetful and need to be reminded many times about this. Some of them do not want to pick up rubbish because it is dirty. Explain how they will transform the rubbish into exciting artworks.

We put all the materials together into big cardboard boxes so that the children can share them.

Some children do not like to overlap shapes. They try to be "neat" by keeping shapes separate. We show them how exciting it is to overlap shapes and colours.

Young children tend to rush the glueing. They sometimes apply far too much glue and their works become wet and soggy. Often they do not stick pieces down firmly and leave pieces loosely attached. We demonstrate glueing and encourage patience.

This technique is very good for teaching children about composition, positive and negative shapes, overlapping, colour and tonal contrasts and especially texture.

## Extra ideas for waste material collage

- You can combine waste material collage with powder paint, oil pastels and dyes to create exciting mixed-media works.
- You can make cloth collages using only pieces of fabric glued onto a piece of firm cardboard.
- Cardboard relief collages are made with pieces of cardboard boxes. You can use the middle corrugated part of the cardboard or the flat surface. Cut interesting shapes, glue them onto a cardboard base and then paint them brightly.

### Ideas for subject matter

Scenes with lots of activities, colourful details and interesting textures e.g. the supermarket, local cafe, petrol station, taxi rank, fruitsellers, my street, my home, the park, the city, the stadium, a birthday party.

Faces and figures.

Still life of objects with interesting textures.

Abstract designs e.g. based on a feeling like anger.

Fantasy themes e.g. planets and spaceships.

A face made from waste paper. Age 7. Orlando.

Two girls
playing with a
ball. Waste
material
collage –
paper,
buttons, wool,
fabric. Age 6.
Orlando.

Two boys. Waste
material collage –
paper, buttons,
wool, fabric.
Age 7. Orlando.

A landscape.
Natural materials
collage – soil,
sand, leaves and
paint.
Age 8. Mofolo.

A landscape.
Natural materials
collage – soil,
sand, straw,
leaves and paint.
Age 11. Mofolo.

# Natural materials collage

*you need*

natural materials
strong paper or cardboard
strong glue
small containers for glue e.g. baby food jars
with lids

1. Work in an area where there is some nature — trees, plants and soil.
   If possible, organise a day trip into the country or work in a nearby park
   or patch of nature.

2. Encourage children to search the area and collect a variety of natural
   materials e.g. leaves, soil, small berries, seeds, grasses, flowers, twigs,
   sand, bark etc. Remind them to collect only small objects and materials
   which can stick easily to paper.

3. Children then create pictures by sticking these materials onto strong
   paper or card. Encourage them to glue things down well and to keep the
   surface of their works quite flat.

4. Encourage children to create some big shapes and some small shapes.
   They should place contrasting colours, tones and textures next to each
   other to separate the shapes from each other.

5. The whole page should be covered with natural materials.

6. When they have finished their artworks, children must shake them gently
   so that any extra unglued pieces fall off.

**Age:** Children of 9 years and older cope well with natural materials
collage.

**Time:** We usually use two sessions to complete these collages.
If we have arranged an outing to the country, we make sure that there is
enough time to finish the collages before we go home.

A landscape. Natural materials collage — flowers, grasses, soil, bark, seeds, leaves. Age 7. Katlehong.

86

# What we have experienced making collages from natural materials with children

Children create spontaneously with natural materials. They feel free and they experience artmaking with all their senses, especially their sense of touch. Using all their senses, they can really explore nature and feel part of it.

Children love day trips into the country and they get very inspired. An advantage of day trips is that children can finish their collages in one long session.

We tell children to collect materials and then gather in one area to work. This makes it easier for us to supervise and remotivate, if necessary.

We warn children about poisonous plants or mushrooms in the area. We point out which plants to avoid and explain why.

We usually take a bucket with us because water is not always close at hand. Water is necessary for washing hands.

Glue gets very dirty from soil, sand, clay, berries etc. It is useful to pour small amounts of glue into small containers, one for each child.

Every child should wear an overall because making collages with natural materials and glue is very messy.

Making collages with natural materials is an excellent way for children to explore texture and tertiary colour relationships.

Children tend to stick rocks onto their collages! We explain that it is important to keep the surface quite flat so that the collage is not too heavy and so that it is easy to store.

Collages made with natural materials need to be stored carefully. They should be stored separately because pieces of material fall off and dirty other work. You can lay newspaper between them for protection.

## Ideas for subject matter

Most children make collages based on landscapes – perhaps the natural materials suggest this theme. We encourage them to observe the landscape around them.

A landscape. Natural materials collage – feather, sand, grass, seedpods, seeds, soil, orange peels and paint. Age 12. Mofolo.

87

Portrait of a
friend. Magazine-
piece collage.
Age 13. Diepkloof.

A landscape.
Magazine-piece
collage.
Age 13. Katlehong.

A landscape.
Magazine-piece
collage.
Age 13. Katlehong.

A landscape.
Magazine-piece
collage.
Age 13. Katlehong.

# Magazine-piece collage

## you need

old magazines with lots of colour pages
(Sunday magazines, Pace, Bona, Tribute,
Fair Lady etc.)
glue
cartridge paper (or similar)

1. Children can begin by drawing a quick sketch or design on their paper. This sketch must be very simple – only outlines and no details added. A sketch is not always necessary.

2. Children look through the magazines and tear out areas of colour and interesting textures which are suitable for their particular subject matter. Discourage them from tearing out ready-made images.

3. Children then create their own images and shapes from these magazine pieces. Encourage them to use some large pieces and some small pieces to build up their forms.

4. The whole page should be covered with magazine pieces. Encourage children to glue the pieces closely together so that no underneath paper shows through.

5. Encourage children to place contrasting colours, tones and textures next to each other in order to separate shapes from each other.

**Age:** This technique is only suitable for children of 10 years and older.

**Time:** This collage technique takes a very long time. Detailed magazine collages can take four or even five sessions.

## What we have experienced making magazine-piece collages with children

Magazine-piece collage is a popular technique. The children love tearing out interesting pieces from magazines and creating artworks from them. Some children call this technique "patch-patch".

It is a very time-consuming technique and we find that we have to remotivate children quite often.

Children tend to read the magazines as they page through. This is a big distraction and slows them down. Watch out for this!

Children tend to cut out ready-made images e.g. a whole tree, instead of creating their own images from magazine pieces. Occasionally a ready-made image works well but too many become boring.

Magazine-piece collage designs can look bitty and unclear. Children need to think carefully about how to separate forms and how to make shapes clear. It helps if children draw their designs in pencil before they glue on their shapes.

Magazine-piece collages are especially good for understanding colour relationships.

Some children try to create perspective in their work e.g. a feeling of depth in a landscape. It helps them to know that colours get cooler and duller in the distance.

## Extra idea for magazine-piece collage

A mosaic technique can be used. Children cut hundreds of small *squares* of different colours. Put them altogether in a box to be used communally. Children do drawings and then fill them in with the little mosaic squares of paper. This technique is extremely time-consuming and should only be done with older children.

## Ideas for subject matter

Landscapes and portraits – based on sketches from real life. Abstract designs and imaginary landscapes.

Children making magazine-piece collages, Diepkloof.

Three figures. Acrylic paint. Age 13. Alexandra.

# Painting

Painting is the process of applying paint or coloured dyes from natural materials onto a surface to create a picture or a design. Paint is usually applied with paintbrushes, but fingers, sponges and knives can also be used. A painting can be done on paper, canvas, board or even on a wall. A painting which is painted directly onto a wall is called a mural.

There is a strong tradition of painting in southern Africa. The earliest paintings were made thousands of years ago by the San. They painted onto rock surfaces using natural materials. These paintings document the history of the San, their spiritual practices and their daily lives.

For many years, African women have been painting traditional designs on the walls of their homes. These murals were originally painted with natural dyes and mud, but today commercial PVA paints are sometimes used.

Today many artists choose to express their feelings and ideas by painting with colour on paper, canvas or board. Artists also work together collectively to paint murals. Murals are a powerful form of communication, especially those on outside walls, because many people in the street see them. For this reason, murals are often painted to express protest.

Painting gives children the chance to express their feelings through colour. Most children are natural painters – they use paintbrushes freely and confidently and choose colours spontaneously. Children do not need to be taught colour theory but it is important for teachers to understand basic colour theory when teaching children to paint. You may need to review colour theory on page 28.

Children begin painting with tempera powder paint on paper. We also paint murals with children whenever we have the opportunity – this gives them a chance to work together collectively.

# Painting with tempera paint

*Careful preparation and good organisation are essential in all painting classes, especially with younger children. Our painting classes with younger children are structured differently from our classes with older children. We describe both approaches below.*

## Painting with young children (5 – 9 years)

### How teachers can prepare for painting sessions

1. Cover all the working surfaces with newspaper.

2. Mix a variety of different colours and tones of paint in the containers. Mix the powder paint with water until it is like thick cream. It should be thick but easy to spread. Make sure that it is not transparent or runny. The containers must only be half-full of paint – this will help to prevent spilling. Children will work in groups of about four or five. They will share colours so mix one full set of colours for each group.

3. Sometimes limit the colour range. Decide on suitable colours for the subject matter. Use your knowledge of colour theory to help you select colour combinations. For example, you can use any one of the following colour ranges for a project:

   only primaries mixed with white (pastel colours)
   only primary and secondary colours
   only the tones of one colour
   only warm colours and black and white
   only cool colours and black and white
   only complementary pairs and neutral colours
   only tertiary colours

4. Place one paintbrush in each container of paint (unless it is a finger painting session).

5. Place a container of each colour with its paintbrush on every table. There should be a full set of colours on each table for each group to share.

6. Place one or two jars of water on each table or have a bucket of water available for children to wash paintbrushes, if they need to.

7. See that children are all wearing old shirts or overalls.

*you need*

tempera powder paint – red, yellow, blue, white
a paintbrush for each container of paint
plastic spoons for scooping paint
containers to mix paint in e.g. babyfood
jars with lids or half-pint milk containers with pegs
jars of water
coloured chalk
cartridge paper (or similar)
newspaper
cloths to clean up spilt paint

# The painting process

1. We introduce children to painting by exploring paint in the following ways:
   - [ ] Begin with a finger painting session. Children create free paintings by applying paint with their fingers. This helps them get familiar with paint and builds up confidence.
   - [ ] Use one or two sessions for children to explore texture in free abstract paintings. They should try to create as many textures as possible by flicking, scratching, blowing, dripping, overlaying and dabbing paint onto the paper. Use some of the ideas on page 100.

     After these explorations, children are ready to make paintings based on different themes.

2. Before they begin to paint, children can do quick line drawings of their subject on their paper. They should use coloured chalk or light coloured paint for this. These drawings should be very simple – just outlines without details.

3. When they are satisfied with their compositions, children can begin to paint. They share the colours on their table with the rest of the group. To paint each colour, they must use the paintbrush provided in the container. When they have finished using a particular colour, they must place the brush back in the container for the next person to use. With this method, no time is wasted cleaning brushes, the paint does not become too watery and the colours do not get too dirty.

4. Demonstrate how to wipe excess paint off the paintbrush against the edge of the paint container. Explain that if there is too much paint on the paintbrush, the paint will drip onto their paintings and it will be difficult to paint small areas. Encourage children to wipe excess paint off the paintbrushes each time before they apply paint.

5. Show children how colours merge with each other if you paint close to a newly-painted wet area. Also, show them how colours dirty each other if you paint over an area when the underneath colour is still wet. Remind them to be aware of this while they are painting.

6. Encourage children to repeat colours through their paintings to create unity – to pull the painting together.

7. Encourage children to use some interesting patterns and textures that they discovered while exploring texture in the first few painting sessions.

**Time:** Young children can complete their paintings in one session.

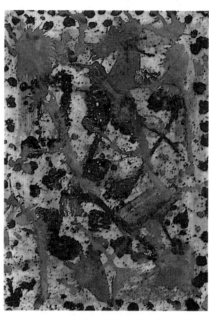

Finger painting with tempera powder paint. Age 6. Diepkloof.

Free exploration of texture. Tempera powder paint. Age 7. Katlehong.

The church. Tones of blue tempera powder paint. Age 8. Orlando.

Casspirs and soldiers in the street. Tempera powder paint. Age 8. Katlehong.

# Painting with older children (10 years and older)

## The painting process

1. We begin with a few sessions to explore the different qualities of powder paint:

   ☐ Encourage each student to experiment with mixing colours. Each student must have his/her own mixing palette, paintbrush and jar of clean water. Each student scoops one spoon of red, yellow, blue and white paint onto his/her palette. Students then mix a wide range of colours and apply these freely onto a big sheet of paper. Remind them how important it is to clean the paintbrush well before applying each new colour. Explain that colours become muddy and dirty if paintbrushes are not cleaned well. They should try to remember how they mixed different colours so that they can mix them again in the future.

   ☐ Students should also experiment with creating different tones of colours. Encourage them to mix many tones of each colour e.g. very light pink – red – dark red. They can add white to colours to make light tones and black to make dark tones. They should mix their own black for this – see page 28.

   ☐ Use one or two sessions for students to explore texture with powder paint. They can use their fingers, paintbrushes, knives, sponges and toothbrushes to create as many different textures as possible in free abstract paintings. See the ideas for exploring texture on page 100.

   After these explorations, students are ready to mix their own colours and to make paintings with interesting textures. They can now begin to make paintings based on different themes.

2. Students can do drawings to base their paintings on. They can also plan their compositions carefully before they begin. They can then sketch their compositions onto the paper with chalk or light coloured paint.

3. Before beginning a painting, each student must mix his/her own range of colours in a mixing palette. Encourage students to mix unusual colours and tones. Tell students to mix their paint thickly – like thick cream or even thicker. To do this, they should add water drop by drop. Explain that paintings made with thin, watery powder paint are dull and lifeless.

4. Discourage students from painting over areas again and again. Powder paint colours lose their freshness and become dull when they are overpainted.

5. Encourage students to use contrasting colours and tones and to repeat some colours throughout the painting to create unity. Also encourage them to highlight some parts with patches of fresh primary colours and colours mixed with lots of white.

6. Remind students to use many different textures in their paintings. They should use some of the textures that they discovered in the early exploratory sessions.

7. If it is possible, sometimes give students the opportunity to paint on very big paper.

**Time:** Free spontaneous paintings can be done in one session. More detailed paintings can take three or even four sessions to complete.

you need

tempera powder paint – red, yellow, blue, white
at least one paintbrush for each student
mixing palettes e.g. polystyrene eggboxes or foodtrays, old saucers or plates, plastic carton lids, pieces of board or masonite
plastic spoons for scooping paint
jars of water
cloths for cleaning up
newspaper
cartridge paper (or similar)
pieces of sponge
old knives
old toothbrushes
found objects to print with

Left:
Finger painting with
tempera powder paint.
Age 10. Diepkloof.

Top right:
Two figures with a
textured background.
Tempera powder paint.
Age 12. Diepkloof.

Bottom right:
A friend modelling.
Tempera powder paint.
Age 11. Diepkloof.

A finger painting of a model. Tempera powder paint. Age 13. Diepkloof.

A woman carrying a tray. Finger painting with tempera powder paint. Age 13. Diepkloof.

## Ideas for exploring texture with tempera powder paint

■ Mix powder paint to various thicknesses, from thin and watery to very thick and crusty.

■ Mix paint with sand, glue, oil, liquid soap or anything else to create different textures.

■ Paint with pieces of sponge. You can attach the sponge to sticks.

■ Paint with sticks, feathers, fingers.

■ Use an old toothbrush to flick paint onto the paper. Try flicking paint over stencils made from cardboard or paper. When you lift the stencil, you will see an empty space where the stencil was.

■ Scratch marks into thick wet paint using the back end of a paintbrush.

■ Pull a paintbrush dipped in very thick paint over an underneath colour. Make sure that the underneath colour is completely dry.

■ Overlay areas of thin paint.

■ Combine paint with chalk, oil pastels, wax crayons, natural materials.

■ Combine paint with collage elements e.g. sweet wrappings, labels, newspaper or magazine pieces, litter.

■ Paint onto different surfaces e.g. sandpaper, hessian, fabric, thick cardboard, brown wrapping paper, black paper, the classified section of the newspaper.

■ Print with the painted surfaces of found objects and cardboard shapes.

■ Paint onto a piece of paper, fold it in half so that the painted surfaces mix together to create interesting textures.

## What we have experienced painting with tempera powder paint with children

Children of all ages love painting but it can be a messy business and painting classes need to be well prepared in advance and well organised. We begin collecting containers and palettes a few weeks before the painting class and ask children to do the same. For younger children, we mix the paints before they arrive. We encourage children who are early for the class to help us decide which colours to mix and to help us mix them.

We find that the first few exploratory sessions are very important for children to get familiar with the qualities of powder paint.

Children often want to do their initial drawings in pencil before they begin to paint – we strongly discourage this. We explain that pencil might show through their colours and that it is difficult to paint with thick paint inside pencil lines.

Many children and teachers tend to mix the powder paint too thinly. Watch out for this!

Muddy paintings must be avoided. Children of all ages need to be reminded not to paint close to or over wet areas and to keep their paintbrushes and water clean. We encourage children to use fresh clean colours.

We encourage children to paint freely and to cover large areas before adding smaller details. We explain that paint is not really suitable for very fine details.

When children are sharing paints at a table, they sometimes knock over a paint container while reaching for another colour. The paint spills and often spoils somebody's work. It helps to talk about being careful and respecting each other's work at the beginning of the session. It is also important not to work in a space that is too crowded and to discourage children from moving around too much.

We sometimes find that older children (12 or 13 years) want to know some colour theory. If they express this need, we introduce them to basic colour theory through practical exercises e.g. painting simple colour wheels or tonal gradation charts. See page 28.

Remember to allow enough time for cleaning up. See that *everybody* helps with cleaning paintbrushes, jars, tables and the floor. Wash brushes carefully until they are completely free of colour. *Never* leave paintbrushes dirty or bristle-side down in water – this is how they get damaged.

If we want to use the paint again, we seal all containers tightly so that the paint does not dry up. We wipe the edges of containers clean and screw on lids tightly or clip down cartons with pegs so that they are airtight.

*Never* place wet paintings on top of each other – they stick together and spoil each other. We lay them out separately to dry while we are cleaning up. They usually dry within half an hour and we then transport them to the storage venue.

## Ideas for subject matter

All subjects can be explored through painting. When preparing colours for younger children, you can mix colours which will enhance the subject e.g.

a fairground – primaries, secondaries and a few neutral colours

a winter evening in Soweto – cool colours and greys

school on fire – warm colours and a few neutrals

a sad event – tones of blue only.

A car accident in my
street. Tempera
powder paint.
Age 13. Katlehong.

The Katlehong Art Centre. Tempera powder paint. Age 13. Katlehong.

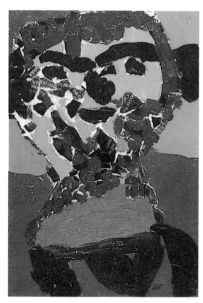

A face. Tempera powder paint and paper collage. Age 8. Orlando.

A face. Tempera powder paint and paper collage. Age 10. Orlando.

A face. Tempera powder paint and paper collage. Age 12. Orlando.

Man on a telephone. Tempera powder paint and paper collage. Age 12. Orlando.

Woman with a hat. Tempera powder paint and waste material collage. Age 12. Katlehong.

# Mural painting

PVA acrylic paint – white, black, yellow, red, blue
a few rollers for painting
coloured chalk
paintbrushes of different thicknesses –
10 cm, 5 cm, 2 cm (one for each container of paint)
lots of empty containers with wide rims e.g. paint tins, canned food tins, jars, plastic containers
long sticks of wood for stirring paint
a screwdriver to open paint tins
a few buckets
plastic garbage bags (one for each child to wear and some to lay on the floor)
newspaper and old cloths
a ladder or scaffolding (if necessary)

## Preparing children for mural painting

1. Begin by explaining to the group what a mural is. Show pictures or slides of murals, if you can. Refer to murals in the immediate area, if there are any.

2. Brainstorm suitable themes for the mural. The group then decides on one theme that they all like.

3. Workshop this theme. Each child does drawings based on the theme, developing detailed and interesting images. Children should work on big pieces of paper to get used to working life-size. Use wax crayons, oil pastels or black paint for these drawings.

4. When all the children are happy with their drawings, cut them out and lay them on the floor or Prestik them onto a big wall. As a group, move the images around into different positions until you have an interesting composition. Use a variety of shapes and heights. Create some busy areas to contrast with simple areas. Remember that you can create a feeling of depth by overlapping shapes, and by placing bigger shapes lower down and smaller shapes higher up in the composition. Discuss how to fill the background and which colours to use in the mural.

5. Talk about working *together*. Explain that each child should work in many areas across the whole mural and not just on one section. Everybody should feel free to paint anywhere. No-one should see a certain part of the mural as belonging to him/her! In this way, individual styles of working and colours are spread throughout the mural. The mural pulls together as one painting – it becomes unified rather than bitty and uncohesive.

6. This workshop process can take a few sessions – it is a very important preparation for mural painting.

## Preparing the wall

1. Check that the wall is not damp, flaky and peeling. If it is, scrape it down until it is a smooth, dry surface.

2. *Prime* the wall – cover it with white PVA acrylic paint. You can apply paint more quickly with rollers than with paintbrushes. Make sure that it is solid white and that no patches of other colour show through. Two coats of paint may be necessary.

3. Wait for the white undercoat to dry. It takes only about one hour.

## Preparing the workspace and materials

1. Lay down groundsheets of plastic. You can cut open plastic garbage bags and spread them out. Cover the ground right up to the wall so that no paint spills onto the floor. On windy days, you need to use stones to hold the sheets down.

2. Prepare an area for paints, containers, buckets and water. This area should be accessible to everyone. Lay down a groundsheet here too.

3. Mix a range of different colours and tones of colours using various combinations of red, yellow, blue and white PVA acrylic paint. (See colour theory on page 28.) Also fill some containers with black PVA paint. Mix the paint in empty containers, using sticks to stir well.

4. Fill buckets with water for cleaning dirty brushes.

5. Make an overall from a garbage bag for every child. Cut away the neck and armholes. The open side of the bag is the bottom of the overall.

A child from PROSCESS children's home painting a mural on the front wall of the home, Hillbrow.

Black painted
outlines of the
mural at PROSCESS
children's home,
Hillbrow.

The mural with some areas painted in colour, PROSCESS children's home, Hillbrow. Painted by a group of children aged 8 – 13 years.

Left:
Black painted outlines
of a section of the mural.
Right:
The completed section.

Children and a staff member from PROSCESS working on the mural.

A close-up view of the central area of the mural.

107

## Painting the mural

1. It is essential that the teacher co-ordinates the mural. S/he should move around, assist children and observe *all the time!* It is important to see the mural as a whole – the links, the relationships between things, the overall meaning and impression.

2. With coloured chalk, each child copies his/her drawing onto the wall in a certain spot. The teacher should show children where to draw, according to the composition plan and the shape of the wall. The drawing should be *big* – children find it quite easy to draw life-size.

3. When the chalk drawings are complete, the children paint the outlines with black PVA paint using brushes about 2 cm – 4 cm wide. Each child should have his/her own container with a little black paint inside.

4. When the children have painted all the black outlines, they are ready to use colour. Wait until the black lines are dry before painting colour!

5. Each child uses one colour at a time. They must fetch the paint from the central area and return the paint and the brush to this area immediately after use.

6. Tell children to paint colours inside and outside the outlines but *never* to cover the black lines. Encourage them to paint broad areas of colour first and to add details later. Remind them to repeat colours throughout the mural to link the mural. They should also leave some big areas of colour without any details to simplify the painting.

7. Do not allow children to change a colour unless the underneath colour is *completely dry*. Avoid too much overpainting.

8. Paints must be sealed airtight when left overnight.

*Age:* Children of 9 years and older cope well with mural painting and they are able to work fairly independently. Younger children need more adult supervision. In a mixed age group, younger children work as partners of older children, helping them wherever possible.

*Time:* We have found three full days sufficient to paint a large mural. We usually use a Friday, Saturday and Sunday. Early on Friday morning, we prime the wall. As soon as the paint is dry, children do their chalk drawings. We spend the afternoon painting all black outlines. We use Saturday to paint most areas in colour. On Sunday we add details and link the mural.

A child working on the mural at Orlando Children's Home, Orlando.

Children painting a mural at Orlando Children's Home, Orlando.

# What we have experienced painting murals with children

Children are natural mural painters. Their paintings are simple and clear and usually have a strong sense of design. They work confidently and spontaneously on murals and do not have the fears that adults have. The adults co-ordinating the mural *must* have confidence in the children. If adults express their fears and shout at children or pass negative comments, the children will lose confidence and the mural is unlikely to be successful. There must be a free atmosphere but also careful co-ordination by the adults involved.

It is important that at least one skilled co-ordinator has an overview of the whole mural and makes linking suggestions. We have found that it is best to have more than one adult helping – at least three adults for twenty children. It is always important that the children make most decisions. All adults involved must be briefed beforehand about their role.

The motivation for the mural is very important. This should not be rushed.

The co-ordinator should check chalk drawings before the children paint the black outlines and remotivate, if necessary.

It is best to prime the wall with white paint rather than any other colour. Other coloured paints show their strongest cleanest colour on a white surface.

It is not always necessary to use black outlines in a children's mural but we have found it the easiest and most successful method. The black lines define shapes, separate forms and link the whole mural together.

The co-ordinators must be on their toes. They need to watch closely all the time to see that children do not destroy each other's images, that they separate forms with different colours, that paint is not dripping and that the whole mural makes sense and pulls together. Mural painting with children is *exhausting* but *very exciting* and well worthwhile. Children love it and their murals are always wonderful.

## Extra idea for murals

If a wall is too textured to paint on e.g. a brick wall, paint the mural onto primed masonite boards. These can then be plugged into the wall when complete.

## Ideas for subject matter

Themes which involve group activities and lots of action e.g. my street, my community, the games we play, our daily activities, the park, people at work, the city.

Imaginary themes e.g. fantasy birds, strange animals, the jungle, outer space, weird cars, trains and aeroplanes, fantasy landscape.

Themes with lots of figures e.g. our families, us, our friends, a big birthday party.

On some walls, abstract designs and patterns are very suitable. Show children pictures of traditional mural paintings for motivation.

Two boys painting black outlines for the mural at Orlando Children's Home, Orlando.

A section of the completed mural at Orlando Children's Home, Orlando. Painted by children aged 8 – 15 years.

A section of the completed mural at Orlando Children's Home, Orlando. Painted by children aged 8 – 15 years.

Inside my kitchen. Lino-cut. Age 15. Katlehong.

# Relief Printing

In all printing techniques, we transfer an image from one surface to another. In relief printing, we make a print from a surface which has relief. This means that some parts of the surface are raised and other parts are low. We apply printing ink or paint to the relief surface – only the raised parts of the surface receive ink. We then press the inked surface onto a piece of paper or fabric and transfer the relief design. By inking the surface again and again, we can make many prints from the same relief design.

Thousands of years ago, the Chinese and Egyptians carved symbols and designs into pieces of wood and pressed these designs into wax or clay to leave impressions. When paper was invented, they inked wooden relief designs and printed hundreds of religious images for mass distribution. These were the first woodcuts and the earliest form of relief printing.

Relief printing has emerged as a strong artform in South Africa today, especially in the townships where many artists specialise in lino-cuts and woodcuts. Relief printing is a popular technique because artists are able to sell many prints of the same design and prints can be sold cheaply and circulated widely. In this way, art is more accessible to the community. Lino-cuts and woodcuts are also sometimes used by community organisations to print pamphlets, posters and T-shirts.

Children enjoy the magic of the printing process. They find it fascinating to transfer an image from one surface to another and they love making many prints of the same design. We explore many relief printing techniques with children. We make found object prints, potato prints, cardboard prints, glue-line relief prints, aluminium foil relief prints, collage prints and lino-cuts.

# Found object prints

## How to print with found objects

1. Collect a variety of found objects with interesting textures and shapes e.g. cork, pieces of tyre, old shoe soles, rubber, buttons, bottle tops, pieces of sponge, leaves, polystyrene, wood, crumpled plastic, cardboard shapes etc.

2. Mix the powder paint with a little water until it is like thick cream. You can add starch to thicken the paint.

3. Paint the surface of each object that you want to print. Paint smoothly and evenly. Do not apply too much paint – only the raised parts of the surfaces must receive paint, not the holes, indentations or grooves.

4. Then press the painted surface of the object firmly onto the paper so that the surface design or texture prints clearly. Notice that only the raised parts (which received paint) get printed.

5. Create an interesting design by combining prints of different found objects. Overlap some prints, repeat some, create patterns. Be aware of positive and negative spaces.

*Age:* All ages.
*Time:* A printed design of found objects can be done in one session.

## What we have experienced making prints from found objects with children

Children get amazed that they can produce such beautiful prints from found objects. They become very excited and before long, they begin printing with anything they can find, including their feet, hands, shoes etc. They soon discover their fingerprints and sometimes start playing detective games! Because of the excitement, children can get out of control and clear limits need to be set.

A few weeks before the project, we ask children to begin collecting interesting objects to print. We then share all the collected objects so that the children can print designs with more variety.

We usually divide the children into small groups. Each group then shares paint for printing and takes responsibility for cleaning up their area afterwards. Discipline is less of a problem when children work in smaller groups.

Children tend to apply too much paint to their objects. This results in messy prints. At the beginning of the session, we demonstrate how to apply an even layer of paint to get a clear print.

Objects need to be washed and dried every now and then. Otherwise the paint piles up and the prints become messy and unclear.

Children must keep their hands clean. This helps to prevent them from printing too many fingerprints when they are holding down their paper to print their objects.

Encourage children to overlap prints and to let shapes touch each other. Also, encourage them to combine different colours – this will make their designs lively and interesting.

This printing technique is very free. With found objects, children can explore textures in a new way.

*you need*

found objects with interesting textures and shapes
powder paint and starch
paintbrushes
cartridge paper (or similar)

## Extra ideas for printing with found objects

■ Water-based printing ink can be used instead of paint. Ink can create clearer and more detailed prints.

■ You can paint layers of dyes or areas of coloured powder paint onto the paper before printing. This creates interesting spatial effects.

■ You can print with found objects onto T-shirts or cloth. Use oil-based printing ink and fix with heat (iron on the inside or put in a spin-dryer).

### Ideas for subject matter
Print with found objects freely to make free abstract designs.
Repeat prints in patterns and place the prints in an ordered way to make clear structured designs.
You can also create imaginary landscapes with found object prints.

A found object print. Age 7. Katlehong.

A found object print. Age 12. Katlehong.

# Potato prints

## How to make a potato print

1. Cut the potato in half.

2. Draw a design on the smooth flat inside surface of the potato half. It is best to use a koki pen for this.

3. With a knife or pair of scissors, cut away some parts of your design. The parts which you did not cut away will now be raised.

4. Mix the powder paint with a little water – it should be like thick cream. You can add starch to thicken the paint.

5. With a paintbrush, apply an even layer of paint to the raised parts of the potato. Do not apply too much paint.

6. Practise stamping your potato design onto a piece of spare paper. Press the potato firmly onto the paper so that the design prints clearly.

7. When you can make clear clean prints, you are ready to create an interesting composition. Repeat the potato print in different positions and patterns. Be aware of positive and negative spaces.

*Age:* All ages.

*Time:* Use one session for children to cut their designs and practise printing. Use another session or two for them to make their final prints.

## What we have experienced making potato prints with children

Children get very excited about potato printing and discipline can be a problem. We find that some children use knives carelessly. We demonstrate how to use a knife carefully and supervise young children closely.

It is best to use new crisp potatoes to get clean prints. We often ask the children to bring their own potatoes.

At the beginning of the session, we demonstrate the whole process – cutting the design, applying the paint and printing.

Remind children that only the highest level of the potato will print. We watch them carefully to see that they do not cut away the parts that they want to print.

If the potatoes are juicy, dry the surface with a cloth before you apply paint. Potato juice can affect the print and make it watery.

Children tend to apply too much paint to the potatoes – this results in smudgy prints.

Before they begin printing, talk to the children about design. Remind them to repeat shapes and to create patterns and to be aware of positive and negative spaces. In their excitement, they tend to print randomly.

We encourage children to use each other's potato designs. In this way, they combine different designs to create prints with a greater variety of shapes.

*you need*

raw potatoes
knives – not too sharp
small scissors
powder paint and starch
paintbrushes
cartridge paper (or similar)

## Extra ideas for potato printing

- Water-based printing ink can be used instead of paint.
- You can fill in the negative spaces between the potato prints with paint or oil pastels to create an overall richness.
- Printing on coloured paper or paper covered with dyes is interesting.
- Other firm vegetables can be cut in half, painted and printed e.g. green peppers, carrots, cabbages etc.
- Potato print designs make beautiful cards and notebook covers.

  You can make also a pencil-holder by glueing a potato print design around a tin. Varnish it for protection.
- Potato print designs on T-shirts and fabric work very well. Use oil-based printing ink for this and fix with heat (iron on the inside or put in a spin-dryer).

### Ideas for subject matter

Potato prints are excellent for structured design projects e.g. designing cloths.

Free potato prints are also exciting – combine contrasting colours and tones. Use overlapping too!

A potato print design.
Age 11. Katlehong.

A potato print design.
Age 12. Katlehong.

A potato print design.
Age 11. Katlehong.

# How to prepare and print with a printing plate

*Found object prints and potato prints are the simplest relief prints. We also explore block-printing techniques e.g. cardboard prints, glue-line relief prints, aluminium foil relief prints and collage prints.*

*For each of these techniques, it is necessary to make a printing plate. We use a block of strong cardboard as a base for each printing plate. On the base, we then create a relief design. We do this by cutting into the cardboard base or by adding raised parts to the base. Only the raised parts of the relief will receive ink. The print is made from the raised design.*

*With older children, we do more complex forms of block-printing e.g. lino-cuts and woodcuts. Here the children carve a relief design into a piece of lino or soft wood. They then print the design.*

*To do any of these block-printing techniques, you need to know how to prepare an inking surface, how to ink a printing plate and how to pull a print. We will describe these steps below.*

## What you need for an inking surface

For an inking surface you can use any one of the following:

a sheet of glass
a smooth masonite board
a baking tray or the lid of a biscuit tin
wax paper stretched and taped over a piece of wood.

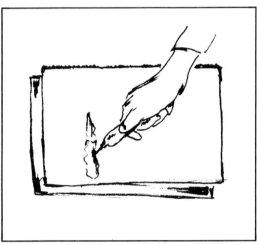

Squeeze a ribbon of ink onto the printing surface.

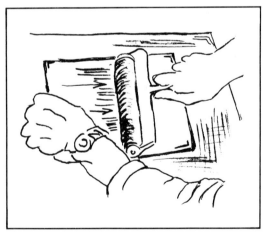

Roll the ink evenly onto the printing plate.

## How to prepare an inking surface

1. Lay down newspaper to protect the table you are working on.

2. Squeeze a ribbon of printing ink onto your inking surface, like you squeeze toothpaste onto a toothbrush. Do not squeeze too much.

3. With a rubber roller, roll out the ink until it is even and tacky (sticky). Roll up and down and sideways.

4. Do not prepare the inking surface in direct sunlight – the ink may dry out quickly.

## How to ink a printing plate

1. You can wear a plastic packet on your hand, like a glove, to keep your hands clean while inking your printing plate.

2. With the roller, roll the ink from the inking surface onto the printing plate.

3. Use even pressure. Roll in all directions – up and down and sideways – so that all parts of the printing plate are well inked.

4. Make sure that there are no pieces of hair, dirt or lumps of thick ink on your plate. The ink on the plate must be smooth and even. Any hairs, lumps, dirt etc. will show on the print.

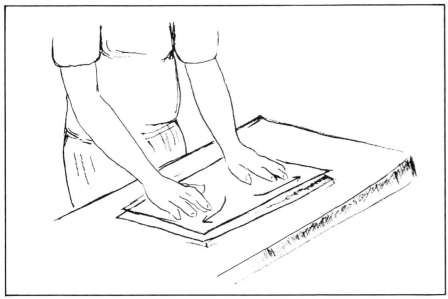

Lay the paper face down onto the printing plate. Apply even pressure from the centre towards the edges of the paper.

## How to pull a print

1. Set aside a special printing area. This area must be separate from the inking area. Keep the printing area spotlessly clean. Make sure that your hands are very clean when you pull a print. It is very easy to dirty prints with fingermarks and smudges, so keep everything as clean as possible.

2. Use a clean piece of paper to print on. The paper should be a little larger than the printing plate.

3. Lay your paper carefully on the top of the plate. The side of the paper which must receive the print must face down onto the plate.

4. Lay the palm of your hand flatly in the centre of the paper on the plate – you will be touching the back surface of the paper. With even pressure, slide your palm smoothly across the paper, from the centre towards the edges of the paper. Do this in all directions. You can also use a roller for this. Make sure that your hands (or the roller) are very clean.

5. Carefully lift one corner-edge of the paper off the plate to see if the print is clear. If not, continue to apply even pressure as before, right to the edges of the paper.

6. Then carefully lift (peel) off the print. Begin lifting at one corner-edge.

7. If you have space, hang each wet print with a clothes peg onto a string – like a washing line. Make sure that the wet prints do not touch each other. Leave the prints to dry. Printing ink takes a long time to dry, especially in cold weather. This can be a problem because wet prints are difficult to transport. If you need to transport wet prints, move them one at a time and lay them out to dry separately. Never place wet prints on top of each other because they will stick to each other.

**Note:** The teacher should prepare one inking surface for all the children to share. Children must take turns to ink their plates and pull their prints. This needs careful supervision. At any given time, only one or two children should be at the inking area. It is a good idea to give children another project to do while they wait for their chance to work at the inking area.

Carefully lift one corner-edge of the paper to see if the print is clear.

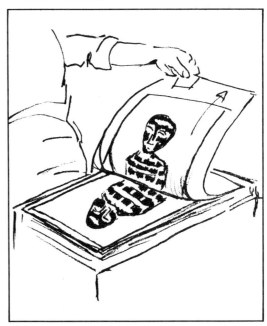

If the print is clear, carefully peel off the print.

# Cardboard prints

## How to make a cardboard print

1. Draw an interesting shape on a piece of corrugated cardboard using a pencil.

2. Cut out the shape along your pencil lines. This shape will be your printing plate.

3. Corrugated cardboard has three layers: a flat bottom layer, a wavy corrugated middle layer and a flat top layer. Add details to your shape by cutting some parts through to the flat bottom layer, tearing the top layer off in some parts, and leaving some parts as they are. The parts which have been cut through to the bottom layer will be the deepest and will not receive ink – these parts will not print at all. The parts where the top layer has been torn off to reveal the wavy corrugated cardboard will print in stripes. The parts which have not been torn or cut away will print solid black.

4. Roll the ink from the inking surface onto the surface of the cardboard shape. Spread the ink evenly and make sure the whole surface of the shape is covered.

5. Lay the shape face down onto the paper to print. Use your hand or a roller to apply strong even pressure on the back of the cardboard shape. To get a very clear and detailed print, turn over the paper and the cardboard shape – hold them together as you do this. Now the paper is on top of the cardboard shape. Apply even pressure onto the back side of the paper.

6. Peel off the paper carefully. See page 119 on how to pull a print.

7. Print different shapes, repeat some, overlap others, create a design. Be aware of positive and negative spaces.

***Age:*** This is quite a difficult technique and is suitable for children older than 9 years. Younger children can print simple cardboard shapes with no details added.

***Time:*** In one session children can design their shapes and cut and tear details. Then one or two sessions are needed for printing.

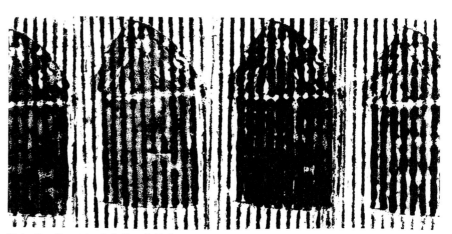

Lions. Cardboard print. Age 12. Dube.

Huts. Cardboard print. Age 6. Dube.

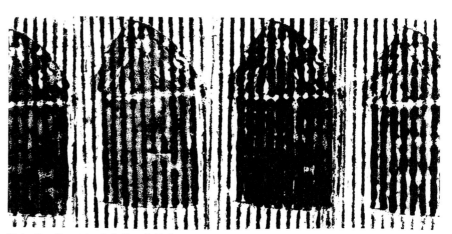

corrugated cardboard from the sides of boxes
pencils
scissors (or cutting blades for older children)
water-based printing ink
rubber rollers
cartridge paper (or similar)
a prepared inking surface (see page 118)

## What we have experienced making cardboard prints with children

Children can print with each other's shapes to create variety. Also, they can all print their shapes onto one big piece of paper as a group project.

Children tend to apply too much pressure when they print their cardboard shapes. The middle corrugated layer gets flattened and the print becomes unclear. We encourage them to press firmly but gently.

Make sure that children's hands are clean when they make their prints.

The cardboard shapes can be printed again and again. But after a while they become scruffy from the wetness of the ink. You can prevent this by painting a coat of varnish on the shapes before printing them.

## Extra ideas for cardboard printing

■ Older children do not need to cut their shapes out. Instead, they can draw a design with many shapes onto one piece of cardboard. Then they can tear or cut away the negative spaces between shapes. They can tear off the top layer of the cardboard and parts of the middle corrugated layer, but they must *not* cut right through the bottom layer of the cardboard. In this way, they create a cardboard relief printing plate.

■ You can paint layers of dyes onto the paper before you print. Then print onto the dyed paper to create interesting effects.

■ If you do not have any printing ink, you can use powder paint mixed with water until it is tacky like printing ink. You can add some starch to get the right consistency. Apply the paint directly onto the cardboard plate using a paintbrush. Work *very quickly* because the paint dries almost immediately.

| Ideas for subject matter |
|---|
| Animals, birds, human figures and abstract designs.<br>Designs based on the letters of children's names.<br>Designs for cloths. |

A monkey. Cardboard print. Age 13. Dube.

A dog. Cardboard print. Age 13. Dube.

A design based on the letter N. Cardboard print. Age 13. Katlehong.

A giraffe. Cardboard print. Age 9. Dube.

# Glue-line relief prints

## How to make a glue-line relief print

1. Draw a design in pencil on smooth cardboard — this will be the base of your printing plate. Keep the design simple and bold — fine details are not possible with this technique. Consider positive and negative spaces.

2. You will now raise some parts of the printing plate with glue lines. With the glue applicator (or the nozzle of the glue container), drip or trail the glue over the drawn lines. Make lines of different thicknesses — this usually happens naturally. The glue lines must be raised because they will receive the ink.

3. You now have a glue-line relief printing plate. Leave it to dry completely. It can take one or even two days to dry.

4. When the glue is completely dry, ink the printing plate well and pull the print. Refer to page 119.

5. If you want the ink in the negative spaces to print, use your fingers and thumbs to press down on the paper between the raised glue lines. The print will have a solid background and a hazy light area around the glue lines. If you want only the glue lines to print, do not apply as much pressure. The print will look more like a line drawing.

6. After applying even pressure onto the back of the paper, turn the paper and the printing plate over (together!) and apply more pressure onto the back of the glue-line relief plate. This gives a clearer print.

*Age:* All ages

*Time:* At least two sessions are needed, one to make the glue-line relief printing plate and the other to do the printing.

*you need*

pencils
strong cardboard without a middle
corrugated layer e.g. shoebox lids,
the cardboard backing of calendars and
foolscap writing pads
glue (cold glue)
glue applicators
water-based printing ink
rubber rollers
cartridge paper (or similar)
a prepared inking surface (see page 118)

A woman and her son. Glue-line relief print. Age 12. Diepkloof.

Two boys. Glue-line relief print. Age 12. Diepkloof.

## What we have experienced making glue-line relief prints with children

This technique allows free and spontaneous expression – the children love it!

At the beginning of the session, we demonstrate how to make a glue-line relief plate. At the next session, when the relief plate is dry, we demonstrate how to ink it and how to pull a print.

If we do not have glue applicators, we use matchsticks or any sticks to apply the glue.

Children tend to rush and their glue lines are often not raised high enough. We encourage them to apply another layer of glue onto some of their lines to make them higher.

Check that children's hands are very clean when they pull their prints.

## Extra ideas for glue-line relief printing

- ■ Glue-line relief prints are very exciting when they are printed onto dyed paper.
- ■ You can also print onto coloured magazine pages.
- ■ You can use paint if you do not have printing ink. See extra ideas for cardboard printing on page 121 for details.
- ■ Older children can make aluminium foil relief printing plates from the glue-line plates. See next section.

> ### Ideas for subject matter
> Free abstract designs.
> Figures and faces.
> Birds and animals.
> Landscapes.

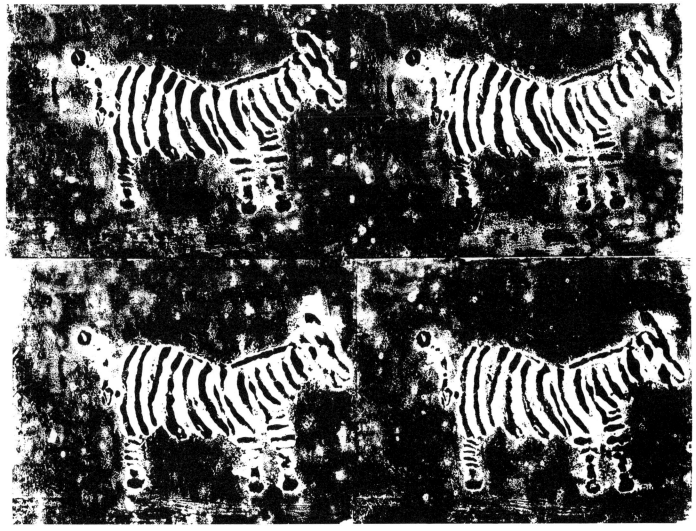

Zebras. Glue-line relief print. Age 11. Katlehong.

# Aluminium foil relief prints

## you need

your glue-line relief printing plate
(see page 122)
heavy aluminium foil (household type)
masking tape (or similar)
blunt pencils
water-based printing ink
rubber rollers
cartridge paper (or similar)
a prepared inking surface (see page 118)

## How to make an aluminium foil relief print

1. Cut a piece of aluminium foil larger than the glue-line relief printing plate – it should be about 8 cm larger on all sides.

2. Lay the foil over the plate with the shiny surface facing up. With your fingertips, press the foil into all the spaces and grooves between the glue lines. It is easiest to start in the centre and work outwards. Then wrap the excess foil around the back of the plate and stick it down with tape.

3. With a blunt pencil point, indent details and patterns in some places on the foil surface e.g. dots, circles, triangles, wavy lines, stars, stripes, spirals. Be careful not to pierce through the foil!

4. Ink the plate and pull a print. Refer to page 119.

*Age:* This is a more difficult technique than glue-line relief printing. Children over 8 years manage well.

*Time:* If the glue-line relief printing plate is ready, one session is needed to cover the plate with foil and add details. Printing will take another one or two sessions.

## What we have experienced doing aluminium foil relief prints with children

We only do this technique after we have made glue-line relief prints. We keep the glue-line relief printing plates to use for aluminium foil printing.

At the beginning of the session, each child inks their glue-line relief printing plate and pulls one print. Children then look at their glue-line relief prints and decide where to add interesting details when they make their aluminium foil printing plates.

It is best if they cover the glue-line relief plate with foil while it is still wet with ink because the stickiness of the ink holds the foil in place.

We make sure that children tape the foil down securely so that the foil does not shift during the printing process.

We demonstrate how to indent details carefully without piercing the foil.

We check that the children's hands are clean before they pull their prints.

We wash aluminium foil plates at the end of a printing session and then use them again.

## Extra idea for aluminium foil relief printing

The aluminium foil printing plates make beautiful artworks as they are. They look even more beautiful when they are polished with brown, red, gold or brass polish.

A glue-line relief printing plate half-covered with aluminium foil on which details have been engraved.

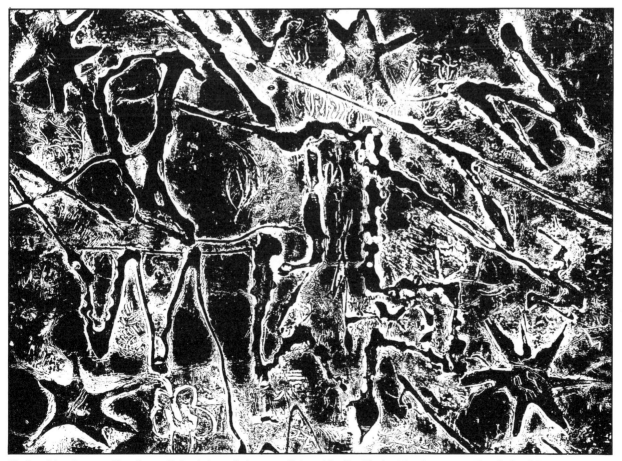
Abstract landscape. Glue-line relief print made by a participant in the Khula Udweba course, Funda Centre.

A collage print. Age 13. Katlehong.

# Collage prints

## How to make a collage print

1. Collect a range of found materials with exciting textures and patterns e.g. vegetable string bags, hessian, corrugated cardboard, string, sand, textured wallpaper, leaves, wire, bottle tops, small lids, paper clips, safety pins, matches.

2. Cut shapes from some of the found materials.

3. Glue these shapes and some of the small found objects *firmly* onto a strong cardboard base. Overlap some shapes, consider positive and negative spaces and create an interesting composition. This collage is your printing plate.

4. The surface of the printing plate will be uneven but it must not have too many different levels. Remember that only the top levels will receive ink and print.

5. Cut a piece of aluminium foil about 8 cm larger than the printing plate on all sides. Lay the foil over the plate with the shiny surface facing up. With your fingertips, press the foil into all the grooves and textures of the surface. It is easiest to start in the centre and work outwards. Then wrap the excess foil around the back of the plate and stick it down with tape. The aluminium foil will prevent pieces of the collage coming off in the printing process.

6. Roll the ink from the inking surface onto the printing plate. See that the ink goes into the grooves and textures of the found materials.

7. Pull a print – see page 119. Remember to use your fingers to press the paper into the grooves and textures – this will give a more detailed and interesting print.

**Age:** Children of 8 years and older can do collage printing.
**Time:** It takes one session to make the printing plate and cover it with foil. Another one or two sessions are needed for printing.

## What we have experienced making collage prints with children

Children love collecting found materials with different textures and arranging them into interesting collages. They also enjoy covering their collages with foil and seeing the textures coming through the shiny metallic surface. The real magic happens when they print their collage plates and see the patterns transferred onto paper.

We ask children to collect found materials with interesting textures and patterns. We place all the materials together and everybody shares them.

We make sure that children glue their found objects *firmly* onto the cardboard before they cover their collages with foil. We also check that there are not too many different levels on their collage printing plates.

When children cover their collage printing plates with foil, they tend to press too hard into all the grooves and the foil tears. We warn them not to glue on sharp objects and we encourage them to press the foil down gently.

Children need individual help when they pull their first print. We show them how to press the paper gently into the grooves to get a detailed clear print. We also make sure that their hands are spotlessly clean!

We use the printing plates many times. It is best to wipe them clean with a damp cloth after a few prints.

you need

found materials with exciting textures and patterns
strong cardboard
glue
scissors
heavy aluminium foil
rubber rollers
water-based printing ink
cartridge paper (or similar)
a prepared inking surface (see page 118)

## Extra idea for collage printing

If you do not have foil, you can give the collage printing plate a coat of varnish before inking it. This will prevent pieces of the found materials from coming loose during the printing process. Leave overnight to dry thoroughly.

### Ideas for subject matter
Abstract designs and landscapes work best.

A collage print. Age 12. Katlehong.

# Lino-cuts

## you need

a block of lino or heavy-duty floor
linoleum
lino-cutting tools
soft pencils
rubber rollers
water-based printing ink
cartridge paper (or similar)
a prepared inking surface (see page 118)

## How to make a lino-cut

1. Make a sketch of your design in black and white. You can do this with pencil or black crayon on white paper. Consider the positive and negative spaces and plan the dark and light areas that you want in your print. Explore different textures, lines and patterns in your design. Remember that the lino-print will be the reverse of your design — its mirror image!

2. When you are satisfied with your design, draw it onto a piece of lino. Use a soft pencil. Shade the areas that you want to print. This will prevent you from cutting away areas by mistake.

3. With the lino-cutting tools, carve out the areas of your design that you want to remain white. Remember that the areas that you do not carve away will receive the ink and print black.

4. Carve interesting lines of different thicknesses, make exciting textures and patterns. Do not carve too deeply into the lino. The low ridges left behind can create interesting textures in places. The prepared lino is now your printing plate.

5. Ink the lino printing plate well and pull a print onto a sheet of paper. Refer to page 119.
   Remember to use a *clean* roller (or the back of a metal spoon) to apply even pressure onto the back of the paper.

*Age:* Children of 10 years and older can make lino-cuts because they can handle the lino-cutting tools carefully.

*Time:* Children can do their sketches in one session and carve the lino in the next one or two sessions. The final printing can take one or two more sessions.

A good position for children to cut lino. This ensures that they will not cut their hands if the tool slips.

My kitchen. Lino-cut. Age 12. Katlehong.

Inside the classroom. Lino-cut. Age 12. Katlehong.

## What we have experienced making lino-cuts with children

We motivate children by showing them lino-cuts and woodcuts made by artists like John Muafangejo, Peter Clarke, Dan Rakgoathe, Phillip Malumise, Dumisane Mabaso, Tony Nkotsi, Sokhaya Nkosi, Shadrack Hlalele, Billy Mandindi, David Hlongwane, Hamilton Budaza, Sydney Holo, Velile Soha. Children get very excited to explore the same technique that many artists use.

Lino from art suppliers is expensive. We buy rolls of heavy-duty linoleum from shops that sell floor coverings.

Lino-cutting tools are sharp and dangerous and they need to be used with care and skill. At the beginning of the lino-cutting session we demonstrate how to hold the lino-cutting tools safely to avoid cutting hands – see diagram on page 128. We keep plasters at hand, just in case!

Some lino is very hard and needs to be softened before carving. Lino softens in direct sunlight so we work outside on sunny days. On cold days, we warm the lino near a heater, if possible.

Children sometimes carve away some areas by mistake. We make sure that they have shaded *all* the areas that they want to print with a pencil or koki pen. Then we remind them not to carve out these areas.

Children tend to over-ink their lino and some carved-away areas get clogged up. We demonstrate inking at the beginning of the session.

We make sure that children's hands are clean when they print their lino-cuts. We also remind them to use *clean* rollers (or spoons) when they apply pressure onto the back of their prints. We speak about the importance of clean prints.

If the children are using letters or numbers in their designs, they need a special reminder to use mirror-writing.

We encourage children to study their first print and look at the balance of black and white. They decide if they want to add more details or carve away more areas. If so, they rework their lino.

We encourage children to make many prints. These can be used later for cards, gifts, exhibitions etc.

## Extra ideas for lino-cuts

■ Try to collect a variety of cutting tools e.g. V's, scoops, flat tools. Encourage children to explore different marks made by each tool.

■ Experiment printing onto different kinds of paper e.g. newspaper, coloured magazine paper, brown wrapping paper, wallpaper, coloured wrapping paper etc.

■ You can do woodcut prints too. Use the same method for lino-cut printing but carve into soft wood blocks instead of lino.

■ Lino-cut prints make wonderful birthday cards, Christmas cards, postcards and calendars.

■ You can also print lino-cuts onto T-shirts and fabric. Use oil-based ink and fix with heat (iron on the inside or put in a spin-dryer).

### Ideas for subject matter
All subject matter is suitable for lino-cuts – see page 19.

My kitchen. Lino-cut. Age 13. Katlehong.

My bedroom. Lino-cut. Age 13. Katlehong.

litter sculpture creature made by a participant in the Khula Udweba course, Funda Centre

# Sculpture

A sculpture is a three-dimensional artwork which you can see from all sides. Sculptures can be constructed, modelled or carved from various materials.

Sculpture is one of the earliest forms of art in Africa. The earliest sculptures were made from wood or clay and had deep spiritual meanings and magical powers. They were used in religious ceremonies and rituals associated with fertility, initiation, marriage, hunting and ancestral worship. Today, in some African communities sculptures are still used in this way. Also, functional objects such as headrests, containers, drums, chairs, walking sticks, spoons and combs are carved with figures and designs and have strong sculptural shapes. In urban areas, this is unfortunately a fading tradition because of the availability of mass-manufactured commercial products.

In South Africa today, many artists still make sculptures from wood and clay, especially in the rural areas where these materials are readily available. Urban artists also work with local materials such as steel, plastic, waste materials and found objects.

It is very important for children to work in three dimensions. When they make sculptures, they develop an understanding of form, volume and space. They also improve their co-ordination skills and learn to solve construction problems creatively.

We mostly use waste materials, found objects and natural materials so that children learn to transform the materials in their own environment. We make wire sculptures, papier mâché sculptures, litter sculptures, woodcarvings and clay sculptures

pieces of pliable wire of different
thicknesses
pliers (as many as possible)
wire cutters

## Extra ideas for wire sculptures

- Parts of wire sculptures can be covered with pieces of thin plastic from coloured plastic shopping bags. Pull the piece of plastic tightly over the wire frame and glue the edges around the frame.

- You can wrap the wire forms with masking tape to make them solid. Wind long strips of tape around the skeleton – cover the open spaces. Then paint and decorate the tape.

- You can wind coloured plastic wire e.g. telephone wire, around the initial wire frame – this adds colour to the sculpture.

- You can wrap fabric pieces around wire figures for clothing.

- Add interesting found objects to the wire sculpture e.g. small batteries, globes, wheels, pieces of leather etc.

- Strips of tin can be wound around the wire form. Old Coke tins and tin from oil cans are good for this.

- Wire mobiles work very well. A mobile is a suspended sculpture. Make about six small interesting wire shapes. Construct a mobile by hanging the shapes with nylon threads from a piece of wood. You can add feathers, corks, bottle-tops etc.

- Children can work in groups to construct very big wire sculptures e.g. figures, buses, aeroplanes.

### Ideas for subject matter

Toys e.g. telephones, helicopters, aeroplanes, cars, buses and bicycles that can move and have figures riding them.
Figures and heads.
Animals, insects and birds.

# Wire sculpture

1. Children collect a variety of wire pieces of different thicknesses, colours and lengths. All wire must bend easily e.g. coat hanger wire, plastic-coated telephone wire, copper wire, electric wire, silver wire, hair pins.

2. Encourage children to experiment with the pieces of wire – bending, curling, spiralling, zig-zagging them. They can make circles, squares, stars and curvy shapes from the wire.

3. Discuss and explore different methods of joining wire pieces together e.g. twisting, binding, winding them together.

4. As a group, brainstorm ideas about what you can make from wire. Each child should choose his/her own subject matter.

5. Discuss wirework in relation to line drawing. Encourage children to combine wires of different thicknesses in their constructions just as they would use lines of different thicknesses in their drawings.

6. Motivate children to add details e.g. seats, headlamps, gear levers in cars.

7. Encourage children to work out ways of making parts of their constructions move e.g. wire wheels that turn, arms that move.

*Age:* Children of 9 years and older can manipulate wire and use pliers easily. Younger children usually need help.

*Time:* Detailed wire sculptures usually take three or more sessions.

## What we have experienced making wire sculptures with children

Children love to work with wire and most children in the townships and rural areas make their own wire toys. They are highly skilled at working with wire and we, as teachers, have only a small role to play when we motivate wirework. In fact, we have learnt many skills from the children – in wirework sessions, they are usually the teachers!

However, the children make more detailed wire constructions in class than at home. This is probably due to motivation and the atmosphere of focused work in the class.

We ask the children to start collecting a variety of different pieces of wire a few weeks before we begin wirework. We then put all the wire together for the children to share.

We encourage the older children to help the younger children with construction problems. This develops a sense of collective work.

Younger children sometimes need help when they handle pliers.

The children have produced some exciting wire sculptures, often with moving parts.

Children love making toys from wire. Children find it interesting to discuss the difference between home-made and bought toys.

A bird. Wire sculpture. Age 13. Katlehong.

A weightlifter and a house. Wire sculptures. Age 14 – 15. Katlehong.

A car. Wire sculpture with found objects. Age 14. Katlehong.

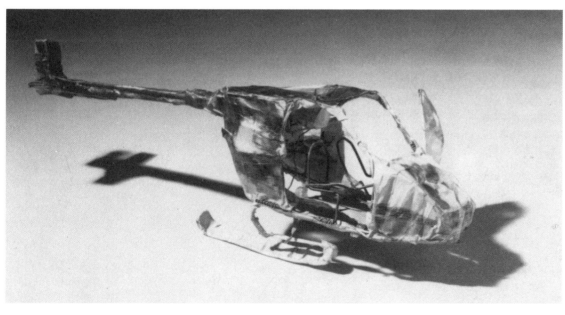

A helicopter. Wire sculpture covered with masking tape. Age 11. Mofolo.

# Papier mâché sculptures with wire frames

## How to make a papier mâché sculpture with a wire frame

1. Using pliers, construct a wire skeleton of your subject e.g a person, bird, insect. Experiment with ways of making the sculpture stand.

2. Take a handful of papier mâché pulp and squeeze out excess liquid. Fill the inside of the wire frame with pulp and model details.

3. Leave the sculpture to dry – this can take a few days.

4. When your sculpture is completely dry, paint it with thick powder paint. Paint interesting details and patterns to suit your subject matter.

*Age:* It is quite difficult to manipulate wire with pliers and to find construction methods to make sculptures stand. So this technique is suitable for older children (11 years and older).

*Time:* You need one session to make the wire sculpture, one session to fill and cover it with papier mâché pulp and a third session to paint it when it is dry.

## What we have experienced making papier mâché sculptures with wire frames with children

The papier mâché pulp is sometimes too heavy for the sculpture frame and the sculpture falls over. We advise children not to use too much pulp. We work individually with children to help them find ways to make their sculptures stand.

These sculptures take a very long time to dry. If they are too solid and thick, they can even get mouldy. To avoid this, we encourage children to squeeze the excess water out of the pulp before they apply it.

Children tend to mix the paint too thinly. We check that the paint is thick and encourage them to paint their sculptures boldly. Sometimes we mix a range of colours beforehand.

## Extra ideas for papier mâché sculptures with wire frames

- You can make papier mâché pulp from the grey cardboard of wine bottle holders or from eggboxes. Shred these and soak them in papier mâché paste overnight so that they become pulp.
- You can wind papier mâché strips around the wire frames instead of using pulp – see page 136.
- You can add wire hooks to these papier mâché sculptures and suspend them to create a mobile.

---

## *you need*

thick strong pliable wire
pliers to manipulate wire
papier mâché pulp
powder paint – mix a range of colours

### How to make papier mâché pulp

1. Make a paste by mixing flour and starch in a big bowl of hot water. Or, you can simply mix lots of wallpaper glue with water in a big bowl.

2. Tear some newspaper into small pieces and add these to the bowl of paste. Add more and more small pieces of newspaper and stir the paste with your hands. Keep adding newspaper pieces until the paste thickens into a pulp. It is best to leave this pulp to stand overnight before you use it.

### Ideas for subject matter

Figures – standing, sitting, playing tennis, dancing, walking a dog etc. Use a circular wire base with a vertical piece of wire to raise the figure off the ground. This will create movement because the figure can bounce on the wire stand.
Animals, birds, insects.

Boys playing soccer. Papier mâché sculptures with wire frames. Age 10 – 15. Katlehong.
Female figures made by participants in the Khula Udweba course.

A bird, a cow, a fly and a bee. Papier mâché sculptures with wire frames. Age 11 – 15. Katlehong.

a variety of cardboard and plastic waste
materials
newspaper strips
papier mâché paste
masking tape
glue
a stapler
powder paint – mix a range of colours

## How to make papier mâché strips

1. Make a paste by mixing flour and starch in a big bowl of hot water. Or, you can simply mix lots of wallpaper glue with water in a big bowl.

2. Tear long thin strips of newspaper about 5 cm wide by 30 cm long. Dip each strip, one at a time, into the bowl of paste. Pull the strip out of the paste and drain off extra liquid by running your index and middle finger down either side of the strip. Use the strip immediately.

# Papier mâché sculptures with waste material frames

## How to make a papier mâché sculpture with a waste material frame

1. Collect a variety of cardboard and plastic waste materials e.g. toilet rolls, milk cartons, matchboxes, wine casks, all sizes of boxes, plastic bottles and containers, cottonreels, cones, balloons.

2. Construct the basic form of your sculpture out of waste materials e.g. a milk carton for a body, a yogurt cup for a head and toilet rolls for legs. Use masking tape, glue or staples to hold the different parts together.

3. When you are satisfied with your basic form, cover it completely with papier mâché strips. Use one wet strip at a time and wind it around the frame. Build up areas where necessary e.g. a hump on a camel's back.

4. The final layer of papier mâché strips must be neat and smooth. When the form is sturdy and complete, leave it to dry. It can take two or three days to dry and a week in cold weather.

5. When your sculpture is completely dry, paint it with thick powder paint. You may want to leave some areas unpainted.

***Age:*** All ages.

***Time:*** It usually takes one session for children to make the waste material constructions, a second session for papier mâché work and a third session for painting and decorating the sculptures.

Two boys painting
their papier mâché
sculptures, Orlando.

## What we have experienced making papier mâché sculptures with waste material frames with children

This project can only be done if you have storage space for wet incomplete works. Some of us cannot do this project with our groups because we do not have suitable storage space.

At the beginning of the session, we encourage children to experiment with different combinations of waste materials until they have created forms that they feel happy with. We never use recipes where all children make a construction of the same subject but we rather encourage each child to make an original form.

Some children have difficulty constructing the frame of the sculpture from waste materials, especially making it stand alone. Children need some individual guidance and it is best to have more than one teacher for big groups, if possible.

We show children how to squeeze out excess liquid from their newspaper strips. We check that they do not use strips which are too wet with paste – otherwise their sculptures get soggy and lose balance.

Young children sometimes need help to create a smooth final layer of papier mâché.

The powder paint must be thick. Children tend to use watery paint so we often mix the thick paint ourselves to avoid this problem.

## Extra idea for papier mâché and waste material sculptures

You can decorate your final sculpture with small found objects e.g. bottle-tops, feathers, nuts and bolts, coloured wire, cotton, wool, cane, cork, plastic, fabric, hessian, leather etc.

### Ideas for subject matter

Figures.

Domestic or wild animals, birds and insects.

Fantasy creatures, strange figures and heads, robots and space creatures.

Vehicles e.g. aeroplanes, cars, buses, motorbikes.

Transport of the future e.g. fantasy cars.

Food e.g. fake cakes.

Bowls and containers. Use a plastic bowl, cardboard box or the base of a bottle to model onto. If you want to remove the bowl or bottle afterwards, remember to smear it with Vaseline or liquid soap before applying the papier mâché.

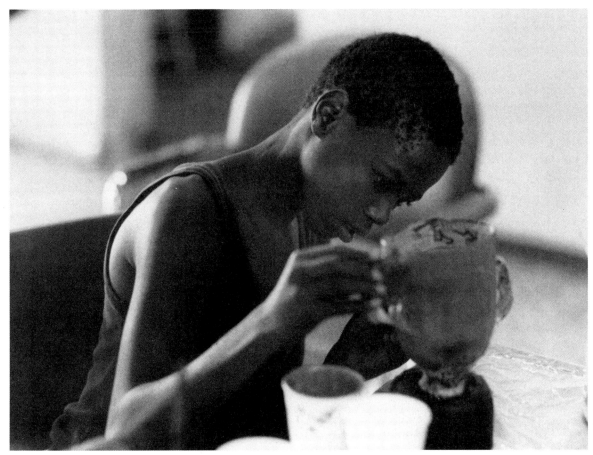

A boy painting his papier mâché sculpture, Orlando.

137

A child painting a papier mâché sculpture on a waste material frame, Orlando.

A woman. Papier mâché sculpture with a plastic bottle for a body, toilet rolls for arms, eggboxes for breasts and a yoghurt cup for a head. Age 8. Orlando.

A pig. Papier mâché sculpture with a plastic bottle for a body, a yoghurt cup for a head and eggboxes for legs. Age 10. Orlando.

Litter sculpture creatures made by participants in the Khula Udweba course, Funda Centre.

## you need

litter and found objects of all sizes, shapes, textures and colours
strong glue
wire
masking tape
stapler
string
pliers
wire-cutters
hammer and nails
papier mâché paste
powder paint – a range of colours
newspaper

# Litter sculpture

1. About a month before beginning this project, discuss litter sculpture with the children. Explain how we can make sculptures from discarded objects and litter and how we can transform rubbish into art. Show examples if you can.

2. Encourage children to begin collecting interesting waste materials from the street, rubbish bins, dumps and junkyards. They can collect plastic tubing, nuts and bolts, small wheels, parts of toys, small machine parts, sieves, handles, pieces of moulded wood, springs, buttons, wire, boxes of various shapes and sizes, plastic bottles, steel wool, hessian, fabric, globes, feathers, wool etc.

3. At the beginning of the first litter sculpture session, each child looks carefully at his/her collection of objects, experiments with different combinations and decides what to make.

4. Encourage children to experiment with various ways of joining different parts. They can use tape, string, wire, glue or nails. They can also use papier mâché strips to bind parts together. See page 136 for how to make papier mâché strips.

5. Remind children to view their sculptures from all sides. All views should look interesting.

6. This project is very challenging and open. There are no techniques to rely on and children have to experiment with all that they know. They have to struggle to create their own personal sculptures.

7. When children are satisfied with their sculptures, they may want to paint them or add small details. Some sculptures are more interesting when they are left unpainted so that their textures show.

*Age:* Younger children can work easily with lighter, simpler materials like cardboard and plastics. These materials are easier to join than metal pieces and wood, which are more suitable for older children.

*Time:* This is a *very slow* project because children take a long time to work out their own construction methods and make their sculptures. We recommend that you organise a holiday workshop to do this project. Use 3 or 4 full days for children to really get involved in this challenging and exciting project. Inform both children and parents well in advance.

A woman. Litter sculpture made by a participant in the Khula Udweba course, Funda Centre.

## What we have experienced making litter sculptures with children

This is an excellent project to develop creative thinking and problem-solving.

Children who are good with their hands respond very positively to making litter sculptures and they find their own creative solutions for difficult construction problems. Other children struggle with construction and need individual attention and advice. But after a while, even these children begin to enjoy construction and find it exciting to solve their problems.

Some children are reluctant to use litter at first. But when they realise that rubbish can be transformed into exciting artworks, they become enthusiastic.

We ask children to bring tools, if possible. We share whatever we have.

Wood glue is best for this kind of construction – wallpaper glue is too weak.

Transporting and storing unfinished works is often difficult. We take great care packing all litter into large cardboard boxes and the unfinished works into separate boxes. We have to spend much time carrying these boxes to and from our venues.

## Extra ideas for litter sculptures

■ Young children can make street scenes using cardboard only. They can use boxes of all sizes and shapes to make houses, buildings, cars etc.

■ Found objects can be put together to make wonderful mobiles e.g. cork, feathers and springs for birds. Hang the forms on nylon threads from a stick.

### Ideas for subject matter

The found materials themselves suggest interesting subject matter. We do not impose subject matter but let each child create his/her own form.

A fantasy horse. Litter sculpture made by a participant in the Khula Udweba course, Funda Centre.

Litter sculpture animals. Age 12 – 16. Dube.

A bird's head, a saxophone and an elephant. Woodcarvings. Age 14 – 16. Katlehong.

# Woodcarving

1. It is best to organise a day trip into the country where there are lots of trees and pieces of wood lying around. Encourage children to search the area for pieces of wood which have interesting shapes or which remind them of familiar shapes. Tell them to be aware of unusual textures and patterns on the wood.

2. With woodcarving tools, they then carve away some parts of the wood to create the shapes they want. Encourage them to also carve patterns, textures and details into the surface of their woodcarvings.

3. Remind children to view their sculptures from all sides while they work.

*Age:* Woodcarving is only suitable for older children (11 years and older) who can handle tools and sharp knives well.

*Time:* Woodcarvings usually take two or more sessions.

## What we have experienced doing woodcarving with children

If we cannot organise a day trip into the country, we ask children to begin looking for pieces of wood a few weeks before starting the project.

Soft wood is easier to carve so we remind children not to choose hard brittle pieces of wood. Wood that is found near rivers is often easy to carve because it has softened from the water.

Children love working with wood, especially in natural surroundings.

We tell children to gather in one area to work so that we can supervise the use of sharp tools and remotivate, if necessary.

We encourage children to bring tools from home, if possible. They then share the tools.

We remind children to think carefully before they carve away areas because when parts have been carved away, they cannot be replaced!

We find that children get inspired when they look at the sculptures of local woodcarvers e.g. Noria Mabasa, Nelson Mukhuba, Jackson Hlungwane, Dr Phutuma Seoka, Johannes Maswanganyi, Lucas Sithole, Jim Ngumo, Vincent Baloyi, Zamokwakhe Gumede, Johannes Segolela.

## you need

interesting pieces of wood to carve
woodcarving tools e.g. chisels, hammers, sharp knives, lino-cutting tools

## Extra ideas for woodcarving

- You can paint parts of wood sculptures using powder paint mixed with water to a creamy consistency. When the paint is dry, varnish the sculptures for protection.
- You can also apply paint to those parts of the sculptures which have carved patterns and textures.
- You can burn some parts to blacken the wood and then carve into the blackened areas so that the natural light colour of the wood shows through.

## Ideas for subject matter

Figures or parts of figures.

Animals e.g. snakes, fish, birds, crocodiles.

Everyday objects e.g. spoons, bracelets, walking sticks.

Abstract shapes and imaginative themes e.g. dragons and fantasy creatures.

A woman.
Woodcarving.
Age 15. Katlehong.

Coiled clay head made by two boys, aged 13 and 15. Dube.

# Ceramics

Ceramics is the art of making sculptures and pottery out of clay. Clay is a natural earthy material which is taken directly out of the ground. It is wonderful to model with because it has plasticity – this means that it can change shape easily.

For thousands of years, children and adults throughout Africa have been working with clay – making their own dwellings, pots, bowls, containers, toys and sculptures. Today, many people still work with clay, especially in rural areas where clay is often easily available. In some areas, it is easier to make functional objects from clay than to buy manufactured goods.

Children create spontaneously with clay and have a natural ability to manipulate it. They enjoy the direct physical feeling of working with clay and they need little encouragement to poke, squeeze, roll and pinch a ball of clay.

It is necessary to prepare clay before use and we explain how to do this on the following page. We introduce children to five basic techniques of working with clay: modelling, pinching, coiling, slabbing and carving. Completed clayworks can be decorated in various ways. We suggest some ways to decorate clay pots and sculptures on page 160.

It is best to heat finished claywork in a special oven called a kiln – this makes the work permanent and strong. This process is called firing. Electric kilns are expensive and seldom available. We explain how to make and use a simple sawdust kiln on page 161. It is important for all children to experience working with clay, even if kilns are not available. We seldom have access to kilns and so we leave the claywork to dry slowly in air at room temperature. Air-dried claywork is quite fragile and needs to be handled carefully.

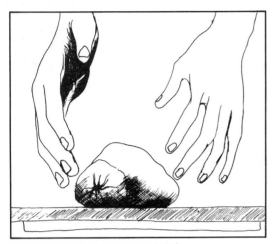

Throw the ball of clay down hard.

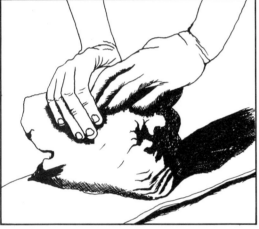

Wedge the clay by pressing down with the heel of both hands and kneading the clay.

## Preparing the clay for claywork

1. Working with clay is messy and children should wear aprons. Each child must have a piece of firm cardboard or masonite board to work on.

2. You can use any available clay with children — even clay from the banks of a river nearby. If clay is not naturally available, we buy modelling clay. We usually use grogged clay with children. Grogged clay contains small particles of already fired clay called grog. Grogged clay is less likely to explode during firing because it is more porous and allows any trapped air to escape.

3. At the beginning of the clay session, give each child a ball of clay and demonstrate how to wedge the clay. It is necessary to *wedge* all clay before using it. This will remove any air bubbles that are trapped in the clay and the clay will mix well. When we wedge clay, we use the same movement as when we knead bread. Throw the ball of clay down. Press down with the heel of both hands and knead. Create a rhythm.

4. After wedging, demonstrate how to cut through the clay in several places to check for air bubbles. Use a piece of nylon thread with a stick on each end to cut through the clay. If there are air bubbles in the clay, you will see little holes. Wedge the clay again a few times to remove the air bubbles.

5. Encourage children to wedge their balls of clay a few times until there are no air bubbles and the clay is well mixed. The clay is now ready for use.

Freely modelled clay heads. Age 13 — 15. Dube.

Freely modelled clay animals and a seated figure. Age 9 — 15. Dube.

# Free modelling

1. Give each child a ball of clay about the size of a big orange. Each child wedges the ball of clay until it is ready for use – see page 146.

2. Encourage children to model small figures, animals or objects in their own free way. If you are going to fire the sculptures, see that the children keep their sculptures small. Air bubbles tend to get trapped in large solid sculptures and this causes them to explode during firing.

3. Allow children to explore their own methods of modelling their clay forms. Some children pull out shapes from the ball of clay, others create a main shape and then add separate parts to it.

4. Explain to children that it is very important to join separate clay pieces securely. Young children can make holes in the clay with their fingers and add parts by inserting them into the holes. Older children can learn how to score on parts – see how to do this in the box below.

5. Encourage children to look at their clay sculptures from all sides. Every view should be interesting.

6. Children may want to decorate their sculptures before or after firing. See page 160 for ideas.

7. When the sculptures are complete, they can be left to dry at room temperature and then fired in a kiln, if possible.

*Age:* Modelling small sculptures is suitable for all ages.
*Time:* Small sculptures can easily be completed in one session.

## *you need*

modelling clay
cardboard or masonite boards
nylon string with a stick on each end
a bucket for moist clay
a bucket for soaking dried-out clay

## Extra idea for free modelling with clay

Children can explore clay without looking by modelling a ball of clay inside a paper bag. In this way, they feel and model the clay directly without seeing their hand or the clay. When they feel that they have made an interesting shape, they can take the clay out of the bag and see what they have created.

### Ideas for subject matter
Animals, fantasy creatures, dinosaurs.
Figures in different positions e.g. lying down, seated, dancing, digging.
Games e.g. chess pieces, dominoes.
Jewellery e.g. beads, earrings.

## How to join clay pieces by scoring

Mix a little clay with some water until it is liquid – this liquid clay is called *slip.*
Apply some slip to the joining surface of each clay piece. Now scratch into the joining surfaces of both pieces of clay. Use any sharp tool to do this e.g. a toothpick or a fork.

Then push the two parts firmly together so that the scratched or scored surfaces join.

Smooth over the join so that it is not noticeable.

# Pinching

## How to make a pinch pot

1. Prepare the clay for use – see page 146.

## you need

modelling clay
cardboard or masonite boards to work on
nylon string with a stick on each end
a bucket for moist clay
a bucket for soaking dried-out clay
plastic to seal incomplete wet claywork

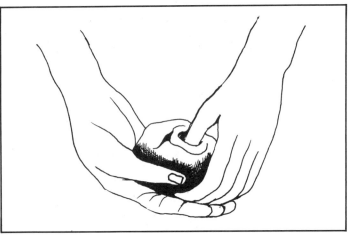

2. Hold a ball of clay in one hand. The ball should be small enough to fit easily into your hand. Press your other thumb deeply into the centre of the ball.

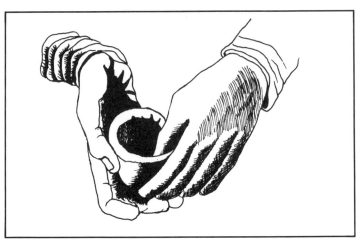

3. Use your thumb to round out the bottom of the pot. Model the walls of the pot by gently pinching the clay between your fingers (outside the pot) and your thumb (inside the pot). As you do this, slowly rotate the pot.

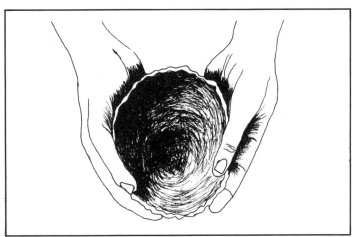

4. Gently push excess clay up the walls until you have a bowl with walls of even thickness.

5. When the pinch pot is complete, leave it to dry at room temperature and then fire it, if possible. Use any of the ideas on page 160 to decorate your pot before or after firing.

6. You can make a lid for your pot by making another shallow pinch pot which can rest on top of your pot.

You can also model a small animal to sit on top of the lid e.g. a snake, bird or lizard. This animal can be decorative or it can serve as a handle to lift the lid.

# How to make a hollow clay sculpture from two joined pinch pots

1. Make two pinch pots which are exactly the same size.

2. Apply some slip to the top edges (rims) of the two pots. Then score these wet surface areas. See page 147 on how to score.

3. Place one pot on top of the other so that the scored surfaces join. The slip helps to seal the join. Use your finger or a flat tool e.g. a sucker stick, to smooth over the join until you cannot see it any more. You now have a hollow clay ball.

4. If the clay is quite wet, you can fill the pots with newspaper so that the ball does not collapse. The newspaper will burn away during firing.

5. It is *very important* to make a small hole anywhere in the ball so that air is not trapped inside it. If air is trapped, the ball will explode during firing.

6. This hollow ball can be made into a head or body of an animal or bird, or a vase or even a musical shaker. Add features and details by scoring on parts.

7. Use any of the ideas on page 160 to decorate your sculpture before or after firing.

**Age:** Children of all ages can make simple pinch pots. Joining pinch pots to make hollow clay sculptures is only suitable for older children.

**Time:** Pinch pots can be made and decorated in one or two sessions. Hollow clay sculptures may take one or two sessions to make. Incomplete works must be covered with plastic and sealed airtight to prevent the clay from drying out.

A pinch pot with a lid. Age 12. Dube.

A pinch pot with incised patterns. Age 10. Katlehong.

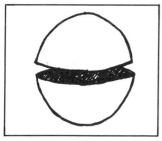

Two pinch pots.

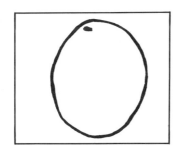

A hollow ball.

A hollow vase.

A hollow shaker with clay beads inside. Push a stick into the ball as a handle.

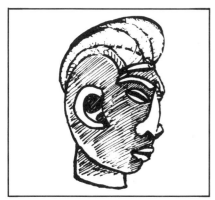

A head on a neck.

A bird.

An animal.

# Coiling

modelling clay
cardboard or pieces of masonite to
work on
nylon string with a stick on each end
tools to smooth clay e.g. plastic knives,
spoons or sucker sticks
a bucket for moist clay
a bucket for soaking dried-out clay
jars to mix clay slip in
a rolling pin (or a bottle or a piece of
wooden curtain rod)
plastic to seal incomplete wet claywork

## How to make a coil pot

1. Prepare the clay for use – see page 146.

2. Make a pinch pot – see page 148.

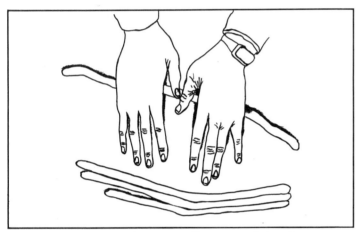

3. Use the palms of your hands to roll sausages of clay. These are the coils.

4. Apply some slip to the rim of the pinch pot if the clay is a bit dry. Lay a coil all the way around the rim so that it rests on top of the pinch pot.

5. Add more coils in the same way to to build up the walls of the pot. If the clay is quite dry, you can use some slip on top of each coil.

6. When you have a few coils, use your fingertips or a tool to smooth the pot walls, both inside and outside. Rub downwards over the bumpy coils until the surface is even. This binds the coils together and strengthens the joins.

7. If you are building a tall pot with many coils, you may need to support the walls with one hand inside the pot. This prevents the walls from sagging under their own weight.

8. When the coil pot is complete, leave it to dry at room temperature and then fire it, if possible. See page 160 for ideas to decorate your pot before or after firing.

To make a lid for your pot, spiral a coil into a saucer shape. You can smooth the surface.

Smoothing the coils of the pot to create an even surface.

Creating a base for the pot with two coils. The pot is upside down.

Smoothing the walls of the pot with one hand inside for support.

# How to make a hollow coiled sculpture

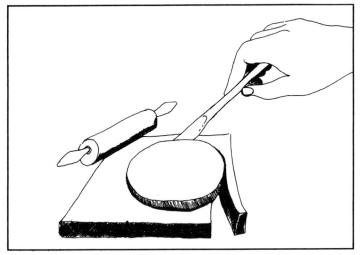

1. If you want a base for your sculpture, use a rolling pin to roll out some clay evenly until it is about 1 cm thick. Cut out a shape for the base of your sculpture e.g. a circle for the base of a neck.

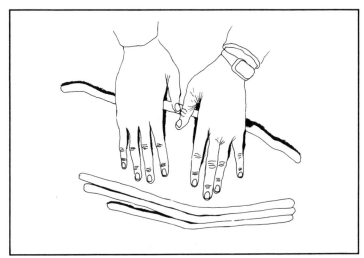

2. Roll some coils.

3. Apply some slip to the edge of the surface of the base. Lay a coil around the edge of the base. Make sure that the coil lies on the slip. Smooth over the join on the inside and the outside.

4. Continue adding coils on top of each other to build up the form of the sculpture. Longer coils will make the form get wider, shorter coils will make the form get narrower.

5. Smooth the coils as you would for a coil pot.

6. Add features and details by scoring on parts e.g. add a nose, ears, eyes and lips onto a head.

7. Remember to make a hole somewhere in your sculpture so that air is not trapped inside. If air is trapped, the sculpture will explode during firing.

8. Use any of the ideas on page 160 to decorate your coiled sculpture before or after firing.

**Note:** You do not have to coil a sculpture onto a flat base. You can begin with a coil for a base and then build up, coil onto coil. The sculpture will be hollow underneath.

**Age:** Children of all ages can make simple coil pots or sculptures. Older children can make large objects with the coiling method.

**Time:** Small pots or sculptures can be made in one session. Large coiled clayworks take quite a few sessions. Incomplete works must be covered with plastic and sealed airtight to prevent the clay from drying out.

## Extra idea for coiling

Four or five children can build a large coiled bowl together. Children should make a flat circular base for the bowl, about 1 cm thick. Each child rolls a few coils and, in turn, adds these to build up the walls of the bowl. Then each child makes a flat figure with outstretched arms (about 1 cm thick) like a gingerbread man. Children score their figures onto the outside of the bowl so that they are holding hands in a ring around the bowl. These bowls look wonderful when they are painted and varnished.

The beginning of a sculpture which will be hollow underneath. The base is a coil onto which other coils will be added.

A pig.
Hollow coiled sculpture.
Age 12. Katlehong.

Freely modelled animals as candle-holders. Age 8. Coiled bowl with snake lid. Age 13. Cape Town.

Coiled bowls decorated with relief figures. Group project. Age 8 — 14. Cape Town.

Cars constructed with clay slabs. Age 13 – 15. Cape Town.

Tape recorders constructed with clay slabs. Age 13 – 15. Cape Town.

Coiled heads with decorative headgear. Age 10 – 15. Cape Town.

# Slabbing

## How to roll a slab

1. Prepare the clay for use – see page 146.

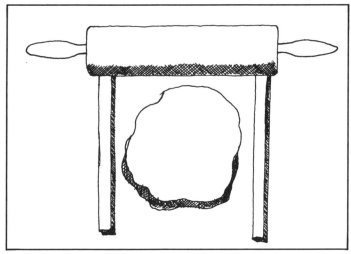

2. Place the two pieces of wood parallel to each other. The distance between them should be less than the length of the roller. Roll out the clay between the pieces of wood. Rest the ends of the roller on both pieces of wood.

3. You now have a flat slab of clay of even thickness (about 1 cm thick).

*you need*

grogged modelling clay
cardboard or masonite boards to work on
nylon string with a stick on each end
tools to smooth clay e.g. plastic knives, spoons, sucker sticks
tools to score with e.g. forks, old toothbrushes
a bucket for moist clay
a bucket for soaking dried-out clay
jars to mix clay slip in
a rolling pin (or a bottle or a piece of wooden curtain rod)
two pieces of wood with straight edges, ± 1 cm thick
plastic to seal incomplete wet claywork

## How to use slabs to construct a box (and other forms)

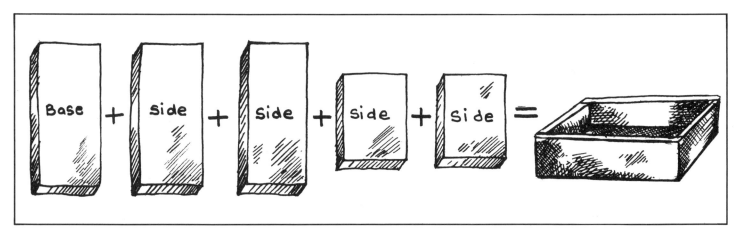

1. To make a box, use a knife to cut out five rectangular or square shapes from one or more slabs of clay. One shape will be the base and the other four shapes will be the sides of the box.

Make sure that the opposite sides of the box are exactly the same size. If you want a lid, cut a sixth shape which is the same size as the base.

2. Leave the slabs to dry for a while until they are firm. It is easier to join slabs when they are leather-hard so that they do not collapse.

3. Hold one side of the box in place on the base and notice which two surfaces join each other.

4. Apply slip to both these surfaces and score them – see page 147 for how to score. Hold them firmly together so that the scored surfaces join.

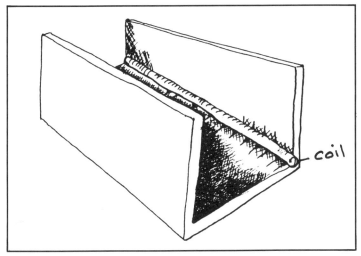

coil

5. Use a tool to smooth over the join on the outside and inside. This helps to bind the slabs together. After joining, place a thin coil along the inside of the join to give extra support. Smooth the coil along the side and the base of the box so that you can no longer notice it.

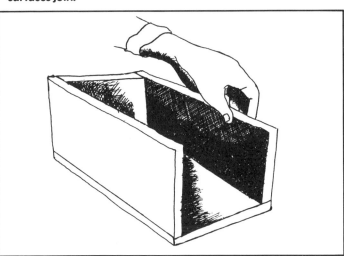

6. Now add the three other sides of your box in the same way. Make sure that all joining surfaces are well scored and all joins are smoothed and supported on the inside with thin coils.

7. Do not think that slabs can only be used to make boxes. The box shape can be transformed into a TV set, tape recorder, bus, car or house. Children can also make figures to sit inside their vehicles. They can even create a whole street scene made out of clay.

8. Leave completed clayworks to dry at room temperature and then fire them, if possible.

**Age:** It is quite difficult to construct clay sculptures from slabs and we only do this with children older than 10 years.

**Time:** Slab constructions can take a few sessions. Incomplete claywork must be sealed with plastic so that it is airtight.

## Other ways to use slabs

- Use a knife to cut out tiles of equal size from rolled slabs. Decorate the tiles using any of the ideas on page 160.
- Younger children enjoy cutting out flat clay shapes e.g. animals, cars, figures. They should use a sharp tool to draw the outlines of shapes on a clay slab and then cut these shapes out of the clay. This is like cutting biscuit shapes out of pastry. They can raise some parts and lower others to create a low relief and decorate the shapes using some of the ideas on page 160.

Figures carved
out of unfired bricks.
Age 9 – 14. Cape Town.

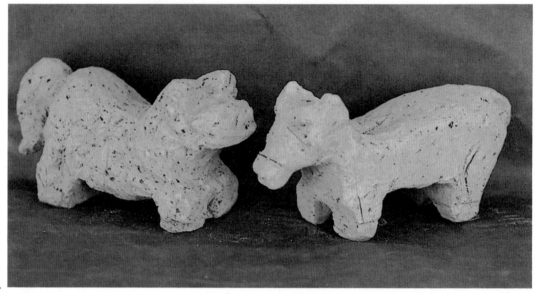

Animals carved
out of unfired bricks.
Age 12 – 14. Cape Town.

Clay relief sculptures.
Age 8 – 14. Cape Town.

# Clay carving

1. Give each child an unfired brick, a knife to carve with and a board to work on.

2. Discuss the difference between modelling and carving. Explain that when you model a sculpture, you build up positive areas but when you carve a sculpture, you cut away the negative areas.

3. Make children aware of how three-dimensional forms look different from the front, back, side and top. Ask someone to pose in a sitting position and all walk around the person, observing and talking about the view from different angles. We sometimes draw a model from different angles on paper before beginning a carving project.

4. Demonstrate how to carve away areas so that a solid form remains.
   – Draw a quick rough design on all sides of the brick before carving. The design must be very simple and contained in the block.
   – Free the form from the brick by roughly carving out the basic shape with a knife.
   – Then carve the details.

unfired clay bricks (from a brick factory)
old metal knives
cardboard or masonite boards to work on
a bucket for excess clay
plastic to seal incomplete work

Drawing on brick.
Front view.

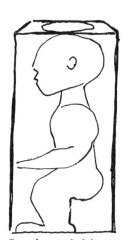

Drawing on brick.
Side view.

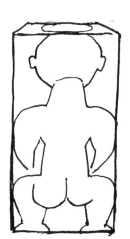

Drawing on brick.
Back view.

Rough shape carved.

Carved details.

5. These clay carvings can be left to dry at room temperature and then fired in a kiln, if possible.

**Age:** Children over 10 years are able to carve in clay.
**Time:** One or two sessions are needed to carve clay sculptures from bricks. Incomplete work must be sealed airtight in plastic.

## Extra ideas for carving

You can make a hollow container from a brick. Carve away parts of the brick to make an interesting solid form. Then cut through the solid form with a piece of wire. Leave both parts to dry in plastic until the clay is leather-hard. Then carve out the inside of both parts so that walls are formed. You now have a container with a lid.

## Ideas for subject matter

Figures can be carved in seated, lying down or standing positions. Standing figures need support e.g. a tree trunk behind their legs.

Tall animals e.g. a giraffe, can be carved into an upright brick. Other animals e.g. a dog, can be carved into a brick lying on its side.

Candlesticks and bookends.

## Ideas for decorating claywork

Claywork offers exciting opportunities for children to explore decoration and pattern. We do not use glazes with children but we choose any of the following ways to decorate claywork:

- Use a sharp tool e.g. a nail or a stick to incise patterns and details into the clay. Do this when the clay has dried and it is leather-hard. This must be done before firing.

- While the clay is still soft, press small found objects into the surface to create relief patterns and textures. Use objects such as bottle-tops, bolts, screws, pegs, rope, leaves, hessian, plastic forks, cork with parts cut away etc. This must be done before the clay dries.

- While the clay is still soft, press natural materials into it e.g. flowers, leaves, seeds. Leave the natural materials in the clay during firing. They will burn away, leaving fine sensitive impressions in the clay.

- If you have white porcelain slip, paint this onto red claywork. Cover the surface completely. Then use a stick to draw through the slip so that the red clay shows through in places. Create line drawings or patterns in this way. This must be done before firing.

- When claywork has been air-dried or fired in a kiln, paint the pots or sculptures using powder paint mixed with water. The paint must be mixed to a creamy consistency and must not be too watery. Acrylic or enamel paint can also be used, but remember that enamel paint can only be cleaned with turpentine so it is not very suitable for young children.

- It is exciting to paint some areas and incise patterns in other areas of the same pot or sculpture. You can also incise into the painted areas or paint the incised patterns.

- You can even use wax crayons or oil pastels to draw onto claywork after it has been fired.

- Claywork that has been painted or decorated with crayons or oil pastels should be varnished for protection. Wait until the paint is totally dry before varnishing.

Young girls painting their clay pinch pots, Dube.

## Firing claywork

Claywork must be completely dry before it is fired. Leave pots and sculptures to dry slowly and evenly at room temperature.

You can make a *sawdust kiln* with bricks as shown in the diagrams alongside.

This firing takes about 24 hours. Somebody should check the fire at regular intervals.

You can get free sawdust from any timber yard.

You can fire clayworks in the same way using a *large tin drum*. Punch holes all over the drum so that air flows freely into the drum to keep the fire burning.

If you have access to an *electric kiln*, make sure that someone who is experienced with firing helps you throughout the process.

## What we have experienced doing claywork with children

Children love exploring, playing and creating with clay and they get very involved in the process. They enjoy feeling the cool clay in their hands. We sometimes tell children to imagine that they are having a conversation with the clay – they can develop their own language with clay through touch. For younger children, the experience of working with clay is more important than the final products which they make.

We teach children the basic technical skills of working with clay but technique is not the focus of our clay sessions. We encourage the children to work freely – clay can be easily reshaped and reworked and "mistakes" can be corrected.

Children love the plasticity of clay. They enjoy making their clay figures or animals walk, dance and move by changing the position of their limbs while the clay is still wet.

Children who struggle with drawing, painting and other two-dimensional artforms often have a natural feeling for working with clay. They enjoy seeing what they have created and they develop confidence. Younger children especially love claywork.

We do not make jars of water available while children are working with clay. If water is close at hand, children tend to use far too much and their clay becomes sludgy and impossible to model with.

If there is no water available at the venue, we take a bucket with us. This water is only for washing hands.

We often do claywork outside. We make sure that children are working in the shade because clay dries out quickly in direct sunlight.

Clay can take from one to three weeks to dry, depending on the weather. Do not leave claywork to dry in direct sunlight because it may crack.

We always use grogged clay for slabbing. This prevents the slabs from warping as they dry.

We always leave lots of time for clearing up when we do claywork inside. We first try to brush or scrape away as much clay as possible from all surfaces. Then we wipe the surfaces with a damp cloth.

Transporting and storing claywork is often difficult. We use tomato boxes, beer trays or cardboard boxes for this. We place crumpled newspaper on the bottom of the box and between the clayworks so that they do not bump each other. It is best to transport work when it is not completely dry. When the clay is very dry, it is brittle and the claywork breaks easily.

Used, dried-out clay should never be wasted. Dry pieces of clay can be soaked in a bucket of water, dried on canvas and then re-wedged. This recycled clay is as good as any bought clay. But you can only recycle clay if it has not been fired.

## How to make a sawdust kiln

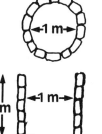

Arrange bricks into a circle with a 1 metre diameter. The spaces between the bricks must be as small as possible. Do not block the holes.

Build up the circular wall until it is 1 metre high.

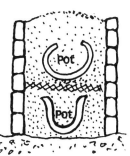

Separate pots for protection with a piece of chicken wire mesh. Surround pots with at least 20 cm of sawdust on all sides.

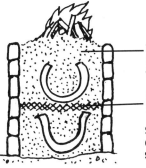

very dry sawdust, half fine and half coarse.

Chicken wire mesh

Start a small fire on top using sticks and paper.

When the flames die down and the sawdust starts burning, cover with corrugated iron and place a few bricks on top to hold the lid down. The fire will move down slowly. There should be a little smoke with a few sparks but no big flames.

After about 24 hours the firing should be over.

# Mask-making

A mask is a construction made to wear over the face. It usually has the facial features of a person, animal, imaginary creature or spirit. A mask hides the identity of the wearer and creates a new identity.

Masks have been used traditionally in many societies. For centuries, people in Africa have worn masks in rituals and ceremonies to act out myths, to teach moral lessons, to solve problems in the community and to entertain. The masks are usually worn with full costume in dances or plays, accompanied by music and song. They often have distorted or emphasized features to express strong feelings.

Remember, masks are made to be worn, not to hang on walls. So it is very important for children to wear the masks that they make in a dance or drama. Children love to see their artworks come alive in this way. Masks provide a wonderful opportunity to link all the arts in performance – art, drama, dance and music. We give some ideas for using masks with movement and drama on page 169.

There are many ways for children to make masks, depending on their age. We explain how to make simple flat masks, paper bag masks and found object masks.

# Simple flat masks

1. Each child decides on a character for his/her mask. Children can describe their character's features and personality to each other before they begin to make their masks.

2. Each child chooses a piece of cardboard, a paper plate or a polystyrene tray as a base for his/her mask. If children are using cardboard, encourage them to draw interesting shapes for their masks and cut them out. It helps to fold cardboard masks down the middle so that they curve around the face.

3. Each child covers his/her face with the base of the mask. Mark where the eyes are with a crayon or a pencil. Children then cut out the eyes of their masks so that they can see through them.

4. Children then paint facial features onto their masks with thick paint. They can also glue on some small found objects e.g. wool, raffia or string for hair and beards, a cork for a nose, matchsticks for eyelashes, pipe-cleaners for eyebrows, buttons for teeth etc.

5. When children have decorated their masks, they attach string or elastic so that they can wear them. They can use a scissor point to pierce a small hole on either side of their masks – these holes should not be too close to the edge. They then thread elastic or string through both holes and knot it securely on both sides. They should measure the length of the string around their heads so that the masks will not fall off.

*Age:* All ages. Younger children (5 – 9 years) cope easily with these simple masks.

*Time:* One session is needed to make the masks and a few more sessions for children to dance or act wearing their masks.

## *you need*

pieces of strong cardboard or paper plates or polystyrene trays
scissors
string or elastic
powder paint – mix a range of colours
small found objects e.g. wool, raffia, string, buttons, beads, bottle-tops, bark, fabric, leather, pipe-cleaners, corks, straws, seeds, feathers, sponges, sticks
strong glue

## Extra ideas for simple flat masks

■ Paper plate or cardboard masks can be decorated with oil pastels or wax crayons and dyes, rather than paint.

■ You can model features with papier mâché onto a paper plate, polystyrene or cardboard base. This also makes the mask sturdier. See page 134 for the papier mâché recipe.

■ Older children can use a flat piece of polystyrene as a base and cut an interesting mask shape with a cutting knife.

## Ideas for subject matter

Heads of animals, birds or insects.

Fantasy creatures e.g. with features of three animals on one head or with features of both humans and animals.

Self-portraits.

Masks which express strong feelings e.g. anger or sorrow or happiness.

Interesting characters e.g. a chief, a witch, a warrior, a sangoma.

Masks based on characters in a story.

Masks based on a theme e.g. hunting, ceremonies, witchcraft.

A mask with a paper plate as a base.

# Paper bag masks

1. Each child decides on a character for his/her mask. Children can describe their character's features and personality to each other before they begin to make their masks.

2. Each child puts a paper bag over his/her head. Mark where the eyes and nose are with a crayon or pencil. Children then cut holes for the eyes and the nose so that they can see and breathe easily.

3. Encourage children to paint interesting and detailed facial features on the front of their bags. They can glue hair on the top, sides and back of the paper bags. For this, they can use wool, raffia, string or newspaper which is curled, folded or plaited. They can also glue on small found objects e.g. feathers for a head-dress, buttons for nostrils or teeth, fabric on the cheeks etc.

*Age:* This is a simple mask-making technique and can be done by children of all ages.

*Time:* It may take one or two sessions to complete the masks, depending on the amount of detail. Dancing or acting with the masks takes a few more sessions.

*you need*

large paper bags e.g. brown grocery bags, potato bags or mealie-meal bags
scissors
glue
powder paint – mix a range of colours
a collection of wool, raffia, string, ribbon, straw, buttons, fabric, feathers etc.
newspaper

## Extra ideas for paper bag masks

- You can use large woven orange bags instead of paper bags. Use stuffed stockings or soft fabric for the facial features and sew these onto the woven bag. You can also knot wool or raffia into the holes for hair.

- Hessian sacks can also be used. Cut out the nose and eyes. Features can be sewn on or painted with powder paint mixed with glue.

### Ideas for subject matter
See the ideas for subject matter for simple flat masks on page 164.

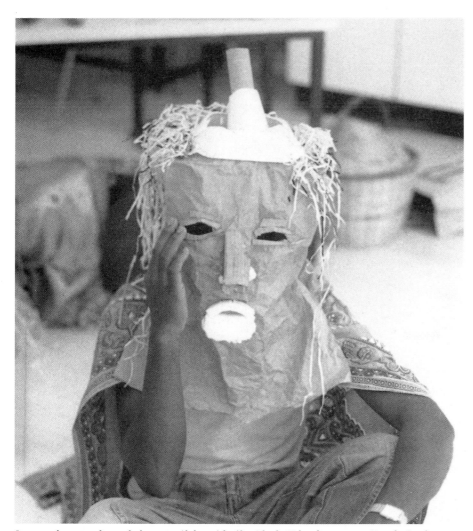

A paper bag mask made by a participant in the Khula Udweba course, Funda Centre.

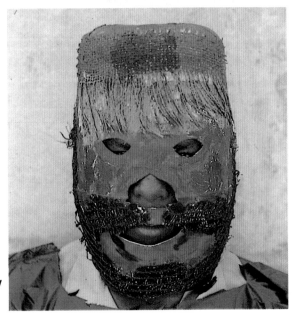
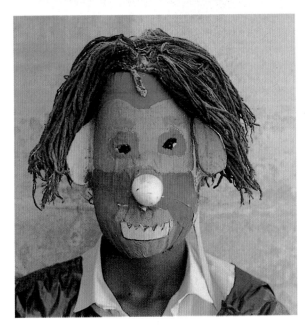

Found object masks made by
children aged 8 – 15 years.
Mofolo and Katlehong.

166

Found object masks made by participants in the Khula Udweba course, Funda Centre.

# Found object masks

found objects which can be used as bases for masks
strong glue
scissors or cutting knives
wire
masking tape
stapler
string
pliers
wire-cutters
papier mâché paste (see page 136 for the recipe)
small found objects for details
powder paint – a range of colours

1. Begin preparation for mask-making a few weeks in advance:
   ☐ Discuss masks with children. If possible, show them pictures of masks and even real masks. Talk about different ways to wear masks e.g. covering the face, over the whole head or held in front of the face.
   ☐ Discuss which found objects can be used as mask bases e.g. cardboard fruit trays or beer trays for masks that cover the face, cardboard boxes which fit securely over the whole head, chicken wire, sieves for masks which are held in front of the face, plastic containers as big as a face (ice-cream cartons) and discarded bowls. Ask each child to find a mask base.
   ☐ Encourage children to begin collecting small found objects, waste materials and natural materials to decorate their masks e.g. buttons, beads, bottle-tops, rope, bark, fabric, hessian, leather, sticks, corks, pipe-cleaners, straws, old stockings, socks, toilet rolls, eggboxes, paper cups, small boxes, small plastic bottles, plastic, steel wool, seeds, sponges, feathers etc.

2. When the children have gathered all their materials, place all the materials in a central spot so that the group can share them.

3. Each child decides on a character for his/her mask. Children can describe their character's features and personality to each other before they begin to make their masks.

4. Each child begins to create features on his/her mask base:
   If the base is a *cardboard box,* children can cut away some areas, glue on small found objects and paint some features directly onto the box. They can even model protruding parts e.g. a nose, in papier mâché onto the cardboard box.
   If the base is a piece of *chicken wire or an old sieve,* make sure that it is large enough to cover the face. It is best to cover the wire base with newspaper strips dipped in papier mâché paste (see page 136). Children should leave spaces for the eyes. They can model protruding features by building up areas of papier mâché. When the papier mâché is completely dry, the mask can be painted and small found objects can be glued on.
   If the base is a *plastic container or bowl,* children can attach found objects for facial features. They can glue on the found objects or they can pierce holes into the plastic base and attach the objects with wire or string.

## Extra idea for found object masks

You can make masks from only papier mâché. Model papier mâché over a round curved object e.g. a bowl, plate, ball or balloon. Remember to cover the object with Vaseline or liquid soap before applying the papier mâché so that you can pull the mask off when it is completely dry. This is not necessary if you use a balloon because you can simply pop the balloon.

5. Encourage children to find their own methods of construction, using all the skills they have learnt e.g. wire manipulation, papier mâché modelling. They must also find ways to wear their masks so that they do not fall off in movement.

**Age:** Making masks with found objects is suitable for children older than 10 years because advanced construction skills are necessary.

**Time:** Making masks with found objects can take two, three or even four sessions. At least two more sessions are needed to wear the masks in a dance or drama performance.

---

### Ideas for subject matter
See the ideas for subject matter for simple flat masks on page 164.

# Ideas for using masks with movement and drama

Begin with some exercises for children to become familiar with their masks:

☐ Ask each child to find his/her own space to work in. Children must not sit too close together. Each child places his/her mask on the floor and sits in front of it, looking carefully at all the details and thinking about the personality of the mask.

☐ Then ask children to put on their masks as if this is part of a daily ritual. They should do this slowly, carefully and ceremoniously.

☐ Then children should slowly feel every part of their masks while they are wearing them. They should feel the textures and shapes and try to imagine the colours.

Play some music and ask children to slowly begin moving while wearing their masks. They should move as if they are the mask creatures. They can begin moving alone and then develop their movements into a dance with a partner. They can then dance in a group of four and finally as a big group.

Encourage children to experiment with different sounds for their mask creatures. They can communicate with each other, calling and answering each other.

Participants in the Khula Udweba course acting in a masked drama, Funda Centre.

169

Sit in a circle and create a basic story together. The story should link all the mask creatures. Then let the children improvise the story while you, the teacher, give some directions as they work. Encourage them to communicate without words — they should use only sounds and body language. Remind them to use big gestures and head movements. Encourage them to use their dance movements and the sounds that they developed.

Children can divide into groups of about six and plan their own dramas to perform for the other children.

These improvisations can be developed into a drama performance for an audience.

Children can make costumes to wear with their masks in the performance. They can paint designs onto plastic garbage bags or hessian sacks using powder paint mixed with glue. Then they can cut away armholes and a neck. Colourful cloths can also be worn as costumes.

## What we have experienced making masks with children

We always begin mask-making with a discussion about why people make masks, how masks are used in rituals and ceremonies and about how they are made. If possible, we show children pictures or slides of different types of masks. We keep this discussion short and simple so that children do not lose their concentration.

We have often noticed that children make masks which are like self-portraits. Their masks seem to reflect their personalities and sometimes even their physical characteristics.

It is important to remind children regularly that they are going to wear their masks. They tend to get so involved in the construction process that their masks become too heavy or impractical to wear. We also remind them to leave big enough spaces for their eyes so that they can see clearly when they wear their masks.

Before children begin painting their masks, we ask them to choose colours which will reflect the characters of their masks.

When children paint their masks, they tend to use thin watery paint. Make sure that the paint is thick — they can add starch to thicken paint. When making masks with younger children, the teacher must mix the paint to the correct consistency beforehand.

We remind children to use contrasting colours or tones for different features so that the features will stand out clearly when seen from a distance. In this way, the audience will be able to see the masks clearly during performance.

Children love wearing their masks in drama and movement sessions. They get very excited and really believe that they are the mask characters. They feel free and uninhibited because they are wearing their masks and have a new identity. It is important for teachers to relax and let the children explore and experience their mask characters freely. We try to be sensitive to their energy and avoid stopping the process too soon. We often join in and dance with the children.

We do not write a pre-planned script for the children but rather let the story unfold during discussion and improvisation.

Those of us who feel unconfident doing drama and dance with the children find it useful to work with drama and dance teachers in our areas. We always ask musicians to play percussion for the movement sessions.

Making masks and wearing them in drama and movement is without doubt a very exciting experience for children and should be part of every art curriculum.

Children dancing in their masks at a movement and drama workshop, Diepkloof.

A shadow puppet show created by children aged 11 – 15 years, Katlehong.

# Puppet-making

A puppet is a figure or doll which is made to perform for an audience. A puppet is manipulated by a person who is usually hidden from the audience. There are many kinds of puppets – glove puppets which are worn on the hand, string puppets which are operated from strings above and rod puppets which are held on rods from below.

For thousands of years, puppets have been used all over the world to amuse, inform and entertain people. There is a rich tradition of puppet theatre in Africa. African puppets are used to enact the lives of great heroes from history, to tell legends and folk tales, to educate and to help people solve problems in the community. Puppets are a very strong medium of communication. Social comment and protest can be powerfully expressed through puppet shows.

Children love watching puppet shows and they relate to the puppets as real characters. They also love to make their own puppets and create their own puppet shows. We teach children two simple puppet-making techniques: cloth glove puppets and shadow puppets. We have chosen these techniques because these puppets do not require drying time and they are quick, easy and cheap to make. We always give children the opportunity to use their puppets in puppet shows.

Cloth glove puppets made by participants in the Khula Udweba course, Funda Centre.

Cloth glove puppets made by children. Age 8 – 12. Mofolo.

# Cloth glove puppets

plain stretchy material e.g. cotton-knit
T-shirt fabric or mutton cloth
pieces of material with interesting designs
buttons, wool
thin cardboard
glue
needles and cotton
scissors
stuffing e.g. old stockings, foam pieces,
cotton waste, kapok etc.

## How to make the body of a glove puppet out of cloth

1. Place your hand onto a piece of cardboard as shown in the diagram. With a pencil, trace the outline of your hand, about 2 cm away from it.

2. Cut out this shape. This is the cardboard stencil for the body of the puppet – the glove.

3. Choose a piece of fabric for the body, perhaps with an interesting design. Fold it in half and place the cardboard stencil on top of the two layers of fabric. Cut out the shape, 2 cm away from the edge of the stencil. Cut through both pieces of fabric.

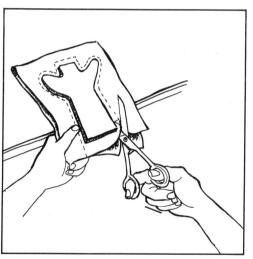

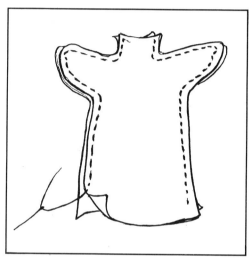

4. Place the two pieces of fabric together with the right sides facing each other. Now sew the two pieces together – one is the front of the body and the other is the back. Stitch about 1 cm from the edge all the way around except across the neck area and the base.

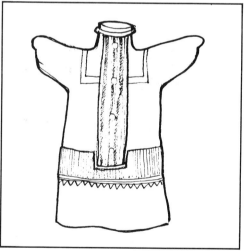

5. This is your basic glove. Turn the glove inside out so that the right side of the fabric shows. You can decorate it by sewing on pockets or buttons or a belt. If the puppet is an animal, you can sew on wool for hair.

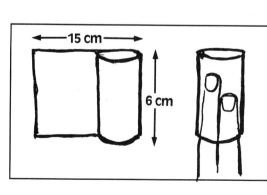

## How to make the neck of the puppet

1. Cut a strip of cardboard which is about 6 cm by 15 cm.

2. Roll the cardboard into a cylinder so that you can fit two fingers snugly into the opening. Glue it firmly.

# How to make a soft cloth head for the puppet

1. On another piece of cardboard, cut out a circle with a diameter of about 20 cm. This is your stencil for the head.

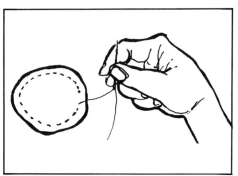

2. Lay the cardboard circle onto a piece of stretchy fabric. Cut around the edge of the stencil.

3. Sew around the circular cloth about 1 cm in from the edge. Use big stitches quite far apart from each other. Sew all the way around but leave a small space between your first and your last stitch.

4. Do not finish off but pull the cotton so the material gathers in. Leave an opening wide enough for the neck cylinder to fit into. Stuff this head with anything soft e.g. foam, cotton waste, kapok. This should now look like a roundish head.

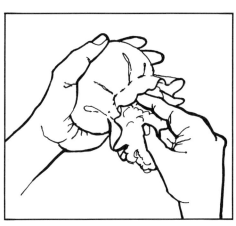

5. Push the neck cylinder halfway into the head. Glue the base of the head onto the neck and before the glue dries, pull the cotton tightly and knot it.

6. Now sew or glue facial features onto the head. Buttons work well for eyes. The nose, lips and ears can be made from stuffed pieces of cloth or stocking. Eyelashes, eyebrows, moustaches, beards and hair can be made from braided, plaited or knotted wool. Make interesting hairstyles, hats, headbands, turbans etc.

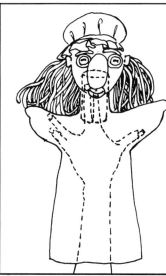

## How to put the puppet together and use it

1. Put the base of the neck into the neck opening of the glove. Glue firmly into place. You can secure the join by wrapping a strip of material or a pipe-cleaner around the neck. This can be a collar or a scarf. The puppet is now complete.

2. To work the puppet, put your hand into the glove. Place your index finger and middle finger deeply and snugly into the neck. Place your thumb into one arm and the other two fingers into the other arm, as illustrated in the diagram.

   You have more control over movement if your fingers can go deep inside the head and arms of the puppet.

3. Experiment with moving the puppet by moving different fingers, your thumb, your wrist and your whole hand.

A stage set up for glove puppets. A plank is balanced between two supports and a blanket is pinned to the plank.

**Age:** As soon as children are old enough to sew, they are ready to make these soft glove puppets. Children older than 8 years can usually sew.

**Time:** The head and neck can be made in one session. A second session can be used to make the body and finish decorating the puppet. Use a few more more sessions for the puppet show.

# Ideas for using glove puppets in a puppet show

Begin by giving children time to explore the possible movements of their puppets:

☐ Encourage each child to move his/her puppet in different ways e.g. bow its head, bend at the waist, cover its face with its hands, raise its arms in surprise, wave goodbye, run, walk slowly.

☐ Ask the children to move their puppets to create different expressions through body language. They can try to make their puppets look depressed, excited, tired, happy, sad, proud, shy etc.

☐ Encourage the children to make their puppets interact with each other. They can hug, wrestle, kiss, hit, hold hands etc.

Children can make characters based on a story that they like. Then they can perform the story in a puppet show.

Children can invent their own puppet characters and improvise a story around these characters.

Children can use cardboard, boxes, papier mâché, wire etc. to make props for the show e.g. houses, cars, trees. They can also use found objects e.g. a real branch for a tree, stones for a rockery, a wire car.

A painted mural on strong paper or cardboard works well as a background scene for the show. Stick the mural onto a wall behind the stage.

A *stage* can be made in any of the following ways :

☐ Balance a plank between two ladders or any other supports. Pin a blanket or cloth to the plank so that it hangs down to the ground. The plank is the stage for the puppets. The puppeteers stand behind the blanket.

☐ Use a table resting on its side. The children stand behind the table and operate the puppets above their heads, on the edge of the table. A bookshelf with a solid back can be used in a similar way.

☐ You can drape a blanket over a washing line. Children stand behind the blanket and operate the puppets at the level of the washing line.

☐ You can make a puppet booth out of wood.

## What we have experienced making cloth glove puppets with children

Children are fascinated by the way that they can transform scraps of material into puppet characters which can move, talk and relate to each other. They become very involved in the whole creative experience of making the puppets and developing a performance.

We collect scraps of materials for the puppets from women's sewing groups or anti-waste fabric shops.

Cloth glove puppets are cheap, quick and easy to make and they do not require drying time. We choose to make them because we do not have storage space for wet unfinished works.

We find it useful to cut cardboard stencils for the glove and head before the puppet-making session. We make a few stencils for children to share.

Some children, especially boys, do not know how to sew. We demonstrate how to use a needle and cotton carefully and keep a check on those who are unfamiliar with sewing. We warn children not to prick themselves.

Puppet-making needs careful explanation – we demonstrate each step clearly.

Children love exploring different movements for their puppets. We always give plenty of time for improvisation.

If possible, we take the children to a puppet show before the puppet-making session. This inspires and motivates the children to make their own puppets.

A puppet made out of a sock.

A puppet made out of a small paper bag.

## Extra ideas for glove puppets

■ You can also make heads for puppets from old stockings or socks. Stuff the toe or foot of the stocking or sock to make a round head. Glue the head onto a cardboard neck and attach to a glove body.

■ You can make heads out of papier mâché. Model facial features out of papier mâché onto a ball of newspaper. When the papier mâché is dry, paint the features with powder paint. Add hair and other details. Attach the head to a cardboard neck and the neck to a glove body. Papier mâché puppet heads are small enough to transport to a safe drying place.

■ You can make sock creatures out of socks. Fit the sock over your hand with the heel over your wrist. Separate your thumb from your other fingers, as widely as possible to create a mouth which opens and closes. Sew on details e.g. eyes, mouth, nose, floppy ears, hair etc. This is a good technique for young children – they should use socks of their own size.

■ Young children can also make puppets out of small paper bags which fit snugly over their hands. They must use new bags which are still folded and flat. They slide a hand into the packet and curve their fingers into the folded base of the packet. They move their fingers up and down to create a moving mouth. Paint eyes and nose onto the base of the packet, add wool for hair and decorate the body.

# Shadow puppets

## How to make a shadow puppet

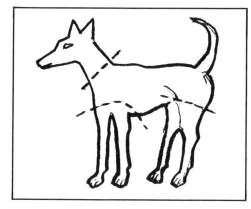

you need

thick cardboard e.g. from
sides of cardboard boxes
scissors or cutting knives
string
thick pliable wire
wire-cutters
paper

1. Draw the outline of the shape of your puppet character e.g. a dog, onto a piece of paper. Cut out the shape.

2. Make dotted lines wherever you want movement to occur e.g. across the neck for the head to move and at the top of the legs for the legs to move. These dotted lines mark the joints of the puppet.

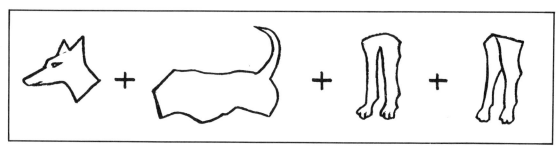

3. Cut along the dotted lines e.g. cut off the head and the legs. You now have four pieces of dog. These are your paper stencils.

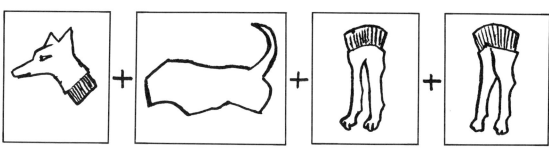

4. Lay each stencil onto a piece of thick cardboard and trace around the shape. These shapes will be joined at the joints so add an extra 2 cm to the joining side of each shape (except the main body). This extra 2 cm allows for overlaps at the joints. See the diagrams below.

5. Cut out the shapes. A cutting knife is easier to use on thick cardboard than scissors.

6. Piece the puppet together by overlapping at the joints. Pierce a small hole through both pieces of cardboard at each overlapping join.

7. Thread a thick piece of string through both holes and knot tightly on both sides. It is best to use a figure 8 knot for this.

8. The knotted string will hold the parts together and will allow movement at the same time. These string knots are the movable joints.

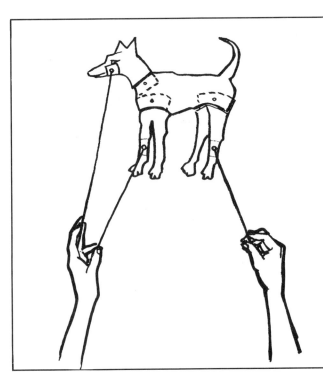

## How to work the puppet.

1. When all the parts are joined together in this way, your puppet will be whole. Now attach long pieces of thick wire to each moving part. You can use masking tape to attach the wire pieces.

2. You move the shadow puppets by manipulating the wires from below. Hold the base of the wires in your hands and experiment with moving your hands up and down and from side to side. Try to make the puppet move slowly and gently and then quickly and jerkily. Make it walk, lie down, run, sit up quickly, stalk, chase etc.

## Ideas for using shadow puppets in a puppet show

In performance, shadow puppets are moved behind a screen with a *strong light* behind them so that they cast shadows onto the screen. The audience in front of the screen sees moving shadows acting out an event or a story. Remember that the room must be as dark as possible.

Shadow puppet shows are often silent and are most effective when there is exciting action and interaction between the puppets e.g. fighting, chasing, stalking, hugging, flying.

Children can choose a story with lots of action and then make characters to act the story out. Or they can create their own figures, animals or birds and then improvise different interactions and happenings.

*Props* can be made for the show e.g. shadow trees, houses, chairs, cars, aeroplanes. These can be cut out of strong cardboard and made to stand.

Make a *screen* by pinning or stapling a piece of white see-through cloth or paper onto a wooden frame. This screen can be balanced on a table or suspended from the roof. You can use a torch suspended from the roof behind the screen to cast a strong light.

*Age:* Making and manipulating shadow puppets with joints is suitable for children of 10 years and older.

*Time:* The puppets can be made in one or two sessions. The shadow puppet show can take one or more sessions.

## Extra ideas for shadow puppets

■ After the performance, children can paint their shadow puppets with interesting colours, details and textures. Painted shadow puppets look wonderful hanging on a wall.

■ Split pins can be used at the joints instead of string knots. Young children can make simple figures or animals with moving joints in this way.

Children manipulating their shadow puppets behind a screen, Katlehong.

180

# What we have experienced making shadow puppets with children

Many children have made their own shadow creatures before by casting shadows of their hands in different positions onto a wall. Some have even explored making shadows behind a sheet to make "movies" for each other. So shadow puppets are not an entirely new concept – they are a development of children's own games and inventions.

Children love making shadow puppets perform behind a screen. They also love watching each other's puppet shows.

Children find it very exciting to make flat shapes move. Making a shadow puppet is like making a drawing come alive!

They sometimes find it difficult to work out where the joints will be. We find it useful to begin the puppet-making session with movement. Everybody bends and moves their joints e.g. wrists, elbows, knees, neck. Then we discuss where the joints are.

Some children find it difficult to understand where to add the extra cardboard for overlaps at the joints. We explain this carefully and give individual help, where necessary.

It is easier to cut through thick cardboard with cutting knives than with scissors. We supervise the use of cutting knives carefully.

We usually use the tip of a nail to pierce the holes at the joints. Scissor points make holes which are too big.

We check that all the string knots at the joints are very tight so that moving parts can hold firmly in different positions without flopping and falling about.

When we do not have a torch to cast a strong light behind the screen, we place the screen in front of a window so that the light from outside shines through it. We make the rest of the room as dark as possible. The children then stand outside the window and manipulate their puppets behind the screen.

A side view of the children manipulating their puppets behind the screen.

The screen is placed in front of an open door. The shadows of the puppets are seen clearly through the screen because of the light outside.

# Appendix A    Information about art materials

## Materials you need to buy

Some commercial art materials are more expensive than others – these are marked with a * in the list of materials below. If possible, phone a few art suppliers in your area to find out the prices of different items before you buy. Prices often differ from shop to shop and money can be saved by finding the cheapest outlet.

Materials must be well cared for and safely stored. Always count materials as you hand them out to the children and check that the same number are returned. Discuss the cost of materials with children and encourage them to take full responsibility for cleaning and storing materials. See that they do not waste materials.

Buy whatever you can afford from the list of materials below.

### Paper

We mostly use cartridge paper because it is a strong white paper and it is suitable for most materials and techniques. It is always cheaper to buy paper in bulk directly from paper factories. Some printing companies are willing to donate off-cuts of paper but these are usually small pieces. Packaging companies are sometimes prepared to donate a roll or two of brown wrapping paper which is useful for drawing, painting and printing on. You can also approach newspaper printers to donate rolls of newsprint, but this lightweight cheap paper is only suitable for drawings and prints.

### Pencils

Buy only soft lead pencils: 6B, 5B, 4B, 3B, 2B, or HB. 6B and 4B are the most useful but, if possible, buy a range of different pencils. Do not sharpen pencils with cheap sharpeners – these eat pencils! It is best if you sharpen the pencils with a cutting knife blade. Pencils are available at stationery shops and art suppliers.

### Wax crayons

Buy some boxes of thick wax crayons (chubby crayons), and some boxes of thin wax crayons which have a wider range of colours. Put all the crayons in a large tin or box so that they can be used communally. Do not leave crayons in the sun because they melt. Crayons can be bought cheaply at some supermarkets and some cafes. They are also available at stationery shops and art suppliers. Some suppliers or factories are willing to donate reject or broken crayons.

### * Oil pastels

These are more expensive than wax crayons. To cut down on cost, it is best to buy children's oil pastels in smaller boxes e.g. 12 colours. Remember that many colours can be created by overlaying a few colours. Store oil pastels in their boxes which have ridges to separate colours. In this way, the oil pastels will not dirty or spoil each other. Oil pastels are available from most stationery shops and all art suppliers.

### Coloured chalks

Buy boxes of coloured blackboard chalk. Children can dip the chalk in sugar water to make the colours more intense. Chalk is available from stationery shops and some supermarkets.

### Coloured dyes

Warm-water or cold-water clothing dyes can be used instead of more expensive watercolour paints or inks. Buy a tin (or packet) of red, yellow and blue dye. If possible, also buy a purple, green and orange dye. Dissolve each tin (or packet) of powder dye in a large jar of water. Warm-water dyes must be dissolved in boiling water and cold-water dyes must be dissolved in cold water. Make sure that you use jars with lids which screw on very tightly. If the jars of dye are sealed properly and stored carefully, they will last a long time. Remember to use dyes with caution because they stain! You can buy clothing dyes at chemists and at some supermarkets.

### Tempera powder paint

Tempera paint is available in liquid and powder form. We buy the powder paint because it can be used to create many different textures. It is only necessary to buy red, yellow, blue, black and white paint. You can mix all other colours from these. It is more economical to buy in large quantities such as 2 kg buckets. You can transfer the powder paint into smaller jars with lids to carry to and from your teaching venue. Large quantities of powder paint are available from art suppliers. Smaller quantities can be bought at stationery shops.

### Paintbrushes

Paintbrushes made from hogshair are suitable for children because they are strong and last for a long time. Buy paintbrushes of medium thickness (no. 10, 12, 14, or 16). If possible, also buy some thicker and thinner paintbrushes. Paintbrushes must always be well cleaned immediately after use and stored carefully. If you store them in a jar, place them bristle side up. Do not allow children to use paintbrushes as glue applicators. Wash paintbrushes regularly in soapy water. Remember that children can use their fingers, sponges attached to sticks or chewed reeds instead of paintbrushes. Paintbrushes are available from stationery shops and art suppliers.

### Wallpaper glue

Buy a few packets of powdered wallpaper glue to use for papier mâché paste and for glueing light materials e.g. paper collages. Wallpaper glue is economical because one packet of powder glue mixes with three litres of cold water. This glue must be mixed 20 minutes before use. It is best to mix only the amount you will need, but the mixed glue can be stored in airtight jars for long periods of time. Children can apply the glue with sucker sticks, sticks or strips of firm cardboard. You can buy wallpaper glue at hardware stores and some art suppliers.

### * Cold glue

Cold glue is white liquid glue which is much stronger than wallpaper glue. It can be used to glue heavier materials together e.g. wood pieces or plastics. It is more economical to buy cold glue in a large quantity e.g. a 5-litre bottle. Pour small quantities into babyfood jars with lids. Glue must be stored in airtight jars otherwise it dries up quickly. You can buy cold glue at hardware stores and at some supermarkets.

### Scissors

Buy children's scissors which have rounded or blunt ends. These are small scissors but strong enough for use in art classes. They are available at stationery shops.

### *A cutting knife

A plastic or metal handled cutting knife with replaceable blades is a very useful tool for an art teacher. This knife should never be used by young children. You can buy a cutting knife at a stationery shop, hardware store or art supplier.

### * Masking tape

Masking tape is very useful but it is expensive. It is mainly for the teacher's use. When children use masking tape e.g. for construction, they tend to use far too much. Supervise them closely to avoid wastage. Buy medium-sized rolls from hardware stores, stationery shops or some supermarkets.

### * Water-based printing ink

This is a very expensive item but one tube can last a long time if it is used sparingly. Water-based printing ink is more suitable for children than oil-based printing ink because the ink can easily be cleaned off surfaces with water. Water-based printing ink is only available at art suppliers.

### * Rubber rollers for printing

Soft rubber rollers (brayers) are expensive but they are necessary for certain printing techniques. You only need to buy one or two small rollers because children can take turns to ink their printing plates. Rubber rollers are available at art suppliers.

### * Lino

It is cheaper to buy heavy-duty linoleum from shops which sell floor coverings. It is sold in big rolls and you need to cut it into pieces yourself e.g. 20 cm x 20 cm. Use a cutting knife to do this. Make sure that you buy soft pliable lino which is easy to cut, not the hard plastic type which breaks easily. Ready-cut pliable lino can be bought at art suppliers but this is more costly.

## * Lino-cutting tools
Buy one lino-cutting tool for each child. The V-shaped tool is the most basic tool but, if possible, also buy a range of different shaped tools. Lino-cutting tools are available at art suppliers.

## Clay
Clay sells quite cheaply at art suppliers and shops which specialise in clay and ceramic materials. It is best to ask for a big bag (25 kg) of grogged modelling clay. For clay carving, ask a brick factory to donate unfired clay bricks.

## * PVA acrylic paint
You only need this paint for painting murals. Buy 5-litre tins from hardware stores. It is only necessary to buy red, yellow, blue, white and black. All other colours can be mixed from these. You always need more white than any other colour. PVA acrylic paint is expensive but some paint companies are willing to donate a few tins for community projects.

## Materials to collect for general use

### Cardboard from the sides of boxes
Large cardboard sheets can be used to press on while drawing (especially when working outside), to make portfolios and to do claywork on. You can get cardboard boxes for free at supermarkets and cafes.

### Masonite boards
These can be used as drawing boards, as bases on which to do claywork, as inking surfaces for printing and as palettes to mix paint on.

**Found utensils** e.g. plastic and metal spoons, forks and knives, sponges, sucker sticks, toothpicks, toothbrushes.
These are useful tools for painting and claywork.

### Cardboard boxes, tomato boxes, beer trays and fruit trays
These can be used to transport art materials and unfinished clayworks and sculptures to and from the teaching venue.

**Large containers with lids** e.g. cake tins, film reel tins, sweet tins, big jars, shoeboxes, strong cardboard boxes.
These are useful for storing loose materials such as wax crayons, pencils, scissors etc. It helps to label the containers.

**Small containers with lids** e.g. babyfood jars, glass jars of all sizes, cottage cheese bakkies.
These are useful for storing dyes and paints.

**Shallow containers** e.g. polystyrene eggboxes and foodtrays, old saucers or plates, baking trays, lids of plastic cartons or cake tins.
These can be used to mix paint on. Old baking trays or the lids of cake tins can also be used as inking surfaces.

**Large buckets** e.g. plastic Atchar buckets, ice buckets, paint buckets.
These are useful for carrying water and for storing clay.

## Natural materials to collect

Many natural materials found in the environment can be used to create exciting artworks. Collecting and using natural materials teaches children to be aware of nature and they realise that they do not always need money to create art.

**For drawing:** burnt wood (charcoal – see page 56), ash, bird droppings, milky plant juices, berries, soil, clay, mud, pollen, powders from mushrooms, crushed leaves or grass and squeezed flowers.

**For painting and dyeing cloth:** natural dyes made by crushing and/or brewing beetroot, tea, aloe leaves, onion skins, ginger roots, coffee beans, marigold flowers, turmeric and potassium permanganate.

**For collage and masks:** leaves, small berries, seeds, pods, grasses, beans, rice, bones, flowers, twigs, sand, soil, bark, feathers, mealie husks and crushed egg shells.

**For printing:** feathers, bark, flowers, leaves, stalks, bones, half fruits and vegetables.

**For modelling or carving:** clay, soapstone and wood.

**For contructions:** reeds, grasses, sticks, thorns, bamboo, bones, wood and fibre.

## Man-made found materials to collect

There are hundreds of different kinds of waste material that can be used for making collages, prints, sculptures, masks and puppets. Both you and the children should search junkyards, dumps and household rubbish bins for "waste treasures" that can be collected for different projects. Below are some suggestions for found objects that you can use.

| | |
|---|---|
| balls (ping pong) | paper clips |
| beads | paper cups |
| bottles (plastic) | paper plates |
| bottletops | pegs |
| buckles | pins |
| bulbs (electric) | pipe cleaners |
| bus tickets | plastic bags |
| buttons | plastic bowls |
| cardboard boxes (all sizes) | plastic cartons |
| cardboard tubes | plastic forks, knives, spoons |
| cards | polystyrene food trays |
| cellophane | polystyrene pieces |
| chicken wire | raffia |
| cigarette boxes | ribbons |
| cloth | rope |
| cones | rubber pieces |
| corks | sandpaper |
| cotton | sawdust |
| cotton reels | screws |
| cottonwool | serviettes |
| doilies | shoe soles |
| eggboxes | sieves |
| foam rubber pieces | socks |
| foil | springs |
| fur | steel wool |
| handles | stockings |
| hessian | straws |
| kapok | string |
| keys | sucker sticks |
| labels | sweet papers |
| leather scraps | tin cans |
| lids of containers | tissue paper |
| linoleum pieces | toilet rolls |
| macaroni | toothbrushes |
| machine parts (small) | toothpicks |
| magazines | torn paintings |
| masonite pieces | toys (broken parts) |
| matchboxes | vegetable string bags |
| matches | wallpaper scraps or samples |
| mealie meal bags (cloth) | wax paper |
| mirrors | wheels (small) |
| moulded wood pieces | wine casks |
| nails | wire (all thicknesses) |
| netting | wool |
| newspaper | wrapping paper |
| noodles | vegetable string bags |
| nuts and bolts | X-ray plates |
| paper bags (brown) | yoghurt cups |

**Appendix B**        **Lesson plan form**              Reference no........................

Date............................................        No. of pupils..............................

Venue ........................................        Age group.................................

Time..................to..................        Teacher......................................

**General educational aim/s**

........................................................................................................................................

........................................................................................................................................

**Specific artistic aims**

........................................................................................................................................

........................................................................................................................................

**Materials**

........................................................................................................................................

........................................................................................................................................

**Technique**

........................................................................................................................................

........................................................................................................................................

**Subject matter**

........................................................................................................................................

........................................................................................................................................

**Motivation**

........................................................................................................................................

........................................................................................................................................

........................................................................................................................................

........................................................................................................................................

**Lesson structure and method**

........................................................................................................................................

........................................................................................................................................

........................................................................................................................................

........................................................................................................................................

........................................................................................................................................

**Ideas for lessons to follow**

........................................................................................................................................

........................................................................................................................................

........................................................................................................................................

........................................................................................................................................

........................................................................................................................................

**Example**      **Lesson plan form**      Reference no... B3

Date.. 2 June 1989      No. of pupils... 16

Venue... Dube      Age group... 9–13 years

Time... 9 am ... to 11:30 am      Teacher...... Maggie

**General educational aim/s**

To develop social awareness. To express ideas about the environment and the community. To work together and share ideas.

**Specific artistic aims**

To work on a large scale. To understand proportion and space. To learn how to unify a group painting by repeating colours, shapes, tones etc.

**Materials**

Tempera powder paint, coloured chalk, paintbrushes, jars + containers, glue, water, litter, masking tape, thick paper – 8 large sheets.

**Technique**

Painting combined with waste material collage.

**Subject matter**

OUR STREET  – a group mural on paper.

**Motivation**

We all go into the street and observe carefully. We close our eyes and listen to the sounds in the street. Inside, we make the sounds that we heard in the street, we discuss everything we saw – we describe things in detail to each other. We talk about shapes, sizes, colours, textures and feelings.

**Lesson structure and method**

Prepare all materials beforehand. Tape 4 sheets of paper together for 2 groups. Ask children to collect litter outside. Motivation for ½ hour. Discuss how to work together on a group painting. Divide into 2 groups. Each group draws their composition with chalk. Children then begin painting and glueing on collage elements. At the end of the lesson, stick the painting onto a wall, stand back from it and all discuss.

**Ideas for lessons to follow**

Another lesson is needed to complete the painting. At the end of this lesson, we will all discuss the final product.

The next few lessons will be used to construct a street scene in three dimensions, using cardboard boxes, corrugated cardboard, corks, plastic containers and found objects. These will be painted.

**Project evaluation form**

Date of project: ..................................................................    No. of pupils: .......................................................

Venue: .............................................................................    Age group: ..........................................................

Teacher: ..........................................................................

Lesson plan reference no: .................................................

1.  Do you think that the aims of this project were achieved? Give reasons for your answer.

    ..................................................................................................................................................

    ..................................................................................................................................................

    ..................................................................................................................................................

    ..................................................................................................................................................

2.  List any problems with the materials and technique used.

    ..................................................................................................................................................

    ..................................................................................................................................................

    ..................................................................................................................................................

    ..................................................................................................................................................

3.  Was the subject matter suitable for this group? Give reasons for your answer.

    ..................................................................................................................................................

    ..................................................................................................................................................

    ..................................................................................................................................................

    ..................................................................................................................................................

4.  Describe the pupils' responses to the motivation method used. Was this method successful? Why/
    Why not?

    ..................................................................................................................................................

    ..................................................................................................................................................

    ..................................................................................................................................................

    ..................................................................................................................................................

    ..................................................................................................................................................

    ..................................................................................................................................................

5. List any problems with the structure and organisation of your lesson/s. Suggest changes you would make when planning this project again.

......................................................................................................................

......................................................................................................................

......................................................................................................................

......................................................................................................................

......................................................................................................................

6. Describe the pupils' attitudes and involvement during the project.

......................................................................................................................

......................................................................................................................

......................................................................................................................

......................................................................................................................

7. Write down all the *positive* aspects of the work produced in this project.

......................................................................................................................

......................................................................................................................

......................................................................................................................

......................................................................................................................

8. Write down all the *negative* aspects of the work produced in this project.

......................................................................................................................

......................................................................................................................

......................................................................................................................

......................................................................................................................

9. Comment on your discussion of the work with the pupils. How did they feel about their own work?

......................................................................................................................

......................................................................................................................

......................................................................................................................

......................................................................................................................

10. Comment on your role as facilitator of this project.

......................................................................................................................

......................................................................................................................

......................................................................................................................

## Appendix D     A list of useful books and journals

### Books about art and artists in Africa

These are available at art libraries and some bookshops.

Asihene, E.V.     *Introduction to the Traditional Art of West Africa.* London: Constable 1972

Battiss, W., Grossert, F. and Junod, H.
*The Art of Africa.* Pietermaritzburg: Shuter and Shooter 1958

Brain, R.     *Art and Society in Africa.* London : Longman 1980

de Lange, J.     *The Art and Peoples of Black Africa.* New York : Dutton 1974

Gillon, W.     *A Short History of African Art.* London : Viking 1986

Johannesburg Art Gallery.
*The Neglected Tradition.* Essay by S.Sack 1988

Lindop, B.     *Gerard Sekoto.* Johannesburg : Dictum 1988

Manaka, M.     *Echoes of African Art.* Johannesburg : Skotaville 1987

Mount, M.W.     *African Art : The Years since 1920.* Newton Abbot : David & Charles 1973

Nettleton, A. and Hammond-Tooke, W.D.
*Ten Years of Collecting (1979-1989).* University of Witwatersrand Art Galleries 1989

Nettleton, A. and Hammond-Tooke, W.D.
*African Art of Southern Africa : Tradition to Township.* Johannesburg : Donker 1989

Thompson, R.F.     *African Art in Motion.* Los Angeles : California University Press 1974

Willett, F.     *African Art.* London : Thames and Hudson 1971

Younge, G.     *Art of the South African Townships.* London: Thames and Hudson 1988

### Useful journals

These are available at art libraries and some bookshops. You can subscribe to these journals by writing to the addresses below.

*ADA*     P.O.Box 16093, Vlaeberg 8018, Cape Town

*African Arts*     African Studies Center, University of California, Los Angeles, California 90024, U.S.A.

*Artlook*     (only back issues are available.)

*Staffrider*     P.O.Box 31134, Braamfontein 2017, Johannesburg

### Useful books for art teachers

These are available at art libraries and some bookshops.

Barnett, R.R.     *Let Out the Sunshine.* Iowa : Wm C. Brown Company Publishers 1981

Dewey, J.     *Art as Experience.* New York : Capricorn/Putnam 1958

Edwards, B.     *Drawing on the Right Side of the Brain.* London : Fontana/Collins 1984

Eisner, E.W.     *Educating Artistic Vision.* New York : Macmillan 1972

Feldman, E.F.     *Becoming Human through Art.* New Jersey : Prentice Hall 1970

Hurwitz, S.     *The Joyous Vision, A Source Book.* New Jersey : Prentice Hall 1977

Lowenfeld, V.     *Creative and Mental Growth.* New York : Macmillan 1975

McFee, J. and Degge, K.     *Art, Culture and Environment.* California : Wadsworth 1971

Talabi, G.     *Art Teaching in African Schools.* Lagos : Heinemann Educational Books 1979

Wachowiak, F.     *Emphasis Art.* New York : Harper and Row 1977

Zdenek, M.     *The Right Brain Experience.* London : Corgi Books 1986

### Some magazines to use as resources

These magazines are all produced in South Africa. They are available in some bookshops or you can subscribe by writing to the addresses below.

*Learn and Teach*     P.O.Box 11074, Johannesburg 2000

*Molo Songololo*     Community House, 41 Salt River Road, Salt River 7925, Cape Town

*The Child*     Education Communications, P.O.Box 41917, Craighall 2024, Johannesburg

*Upbeat*     P.O.Box 11350, Johannesburg 2000

Shoes constructed with
clay slabs. Age 13. Dube.

# Appendix E    A glossary of some art terms

**Abstract art** – In abstract artworks, the subject matter and forms are not represented as they appear in real life. Sometimes the content of an abstract artwork is purely imaginative e.g. designs.

**Analogous colours** – Analogous colours are closely related. They are neighbours on the colour wheel e.g. blue, blue-green and green.

**Artform** – The form which an artwork takes e.g. a drawing, a collage, a painting, a print, a sculpture or a mask.

**Art process** – The process used to make an artwork e.g. drawing, painting, printing, collage, sculpting, mask-making, puppet-making.

**Artwork** – A general term applied to any work of art.

**Blind contour drawing** – A line drawing which is made without looking at the drawing until it is complete. See page 38.

**Block-printing** – A form of relief printing where the printing plate is a block of strong cardboard, wood or linoleum which has a relief design incised in it or raised on it.

**Canvas** – A strong fabric (cotton, linen, jute etc.) that is prepared as a surface for painting on.

**Carving** – The process of cutting away parts of a block of wood, stone or other hard material.

**Ceramics** – The art of making sculpture or pottery out of clay.

**Charcoal** – A stick of blackened charred wood used for drawing. See page 56 for how to make charcoal.

**Coiling** – A method of constructing with clay. Rolled clay sausages are coiled (laid in rings) to create a desired shape e.g. a coil pot.

**Collage** – A picture or design made by glueing different kinds of paper, pieces of fabric and textured materials onto a flat surface. Collage comes from a French word "coller" which means "to stick".

**Colour contrast** – Colour contrast refers to the difference between colours. Contrasting colours are used for emphasis in an artwork.

**Colour theory** – Information about the use of colour, about relationships between colours and about how to mix different colours to create new colours.

**Colour wheel** – A circle which shows the relationship between different colours. For example, complementary colours are opposite each other on the colour wheel. See the colour wheel on page 28.

**Commercial art materials** – Art materials which you can buy from suppliers.

**Complementary colours** – Complementary colours make each other seem stronger. For example, red strengthens green because red is the complementary colour of green. Complementary colours are directly opposite each other on the colour wheel.

**Composition** – The way that art elements e.g. shapes, are arranged in an artwork.

**Consistency** – The thickness or softness of a medium or material. For example, paint can be thin or thick, clay can be soft or hard.

**Continuous contour drawing** – A line drawing made with one continuous unbroken line. In a continuous line drawing, the pencil is never lifted off the paper until the drawing is finished.

**Contours** – Lines which define forms.

**Cool colours** – Colours which give off a feeling of coldness or coolness e.g. blues and greens.

**Corrugated cardboard** – Cardboard which has a wavy middle layer with ridges which lie between smooth outside layers. Many cardboard boxes are made from corrugated cardboard.

**Creative** – Having the ability to use the imagination, to express ideas and to present ideas in an individual and effective manner.

**Creative thinking** – Thinking in an original and diverse way.

**Cross-hatching** – A way of creating different tones by repeating and overlapping parallel, horizontal, vertical or diagonal lines. See page 42.

**Dyes** – Man-made or natural colouring matter which dissolves in water and stains paper or fabric permanently.

**Elements of art** – Line, tone, texture, shape, colour, space and composition are some of the elements of art.

**Enamel paint** – Oil-based paint that forms a hard and shiny surface when it dries. When it is dry, this paint suggests the quality of baked enamel.

**Engrave** – To carve, cut or incise into a hard surface.

**Expressive** – An expressive artwork shows the emotions and feelings of the artist strongly.

**Figure drawing** – Drawing the human body while observing a person as a model.

**Finger-painting** – Using fingers to paint with, instead of a paintbrush.

**Firing** – Baking claywork in a kiln (oven) to make it permanent and strong.

**Fix** – Artworks can be fixed to prevent them from smudging or fading. For example, a charcoal drawing can be sprayed with hairspray, or a printed design on fabric can be ironed on its back side.

**Form** – The three-dimensional shape and structure of an object.

**Found objects** – Discarded objects which have been thrown away can be collected and used in artworks.

**Frame** – A border surrounding a picture.

**Functional object** – An object which has a specific use and is not only decorative.

**Gesture drawing** – A loose free drawing with no details. Gesture drawings are often drawn quickly to express a feeling of movement.

**Glaze** – A transparent or coloured coating applied to claywork. Glaze can be used to decorate the claywork and to make it waterproof.

**Grog** – Small particles of already fired clay. Grog can be added to clay to make it more porous. Grogged clay is less likely to explode during firing because trapped air will be able to escape.

**Hessian** – Rough sackcloth.

**Highlight** – A patch of direct intense light.

**Image** – A visual representation of a person, animal, object or idea in an artwork or in the mind.

**Incise** – To cut or carve thin lines into a hard surface.

**Inking surface** – A flat surface on which ink can be rolled out before it is applied to a printing plate.

**Kapok** – A natural fibre which is used to stuff pillows, cushions etc.

**Kiln** – An oven for firing claywork. Electric kilns can be used or you can make your own sawdust kiln – see page 161.

**Koki pen** – A felt-tipped pen.

**Landscape** – A view of outside scenery e.g. trees, roads, rocks, sky, as the subject matter of an artwork.

**Leather-hard** – Leather-hard clay is partly dry but not yet brittle or crumbly.

**Linoleum** – A hard material used to cover floors. Linoleum can also be used to make relief prints called lino-cuts.

**Mask** – A contruction which is worn over the face to hide the identity of the wearer. It usually has the facial features of a person, animal or imaginary creature.

**Mixed media** – Two or more different art materials used in one artwork e.g. wax crayons and dyes.

**Mobile** – A suspended sculpture with parts which hang on wire or string so that they move freely in air currents.

**Model** – A person who poses in a seated, standing or lying position so that other people can draw or paint him/her.

**Modelling** – In sculpture, the process of shaping and manipulating clay or other soft material in order to create a three-dimensional form.

**Mosaic** – A picture or design made from small coloured pieces of cut-out paper (or other materials). The small pieces are placed and glued next to each other on a flat surface.

**Motivate** – To inspire children to want to create.

**Mural** – A painting which is painted directly onto a wall.

**Natural materials** – Materials from natural sources such as plants, minerals and animals.

**Negative spaces** – The areas around and between the shapes or forms in an artwork.

**Neutral colours** – Colours which are not bright e.g. earthy browns, greys, dull greens, khaki, mustard, ochre and other tertiary colours.

**Observation drawing** – Drawing while looking closely at a human figure, an animal or an object.

**Overlay** – To apply layers of colours or materials on top of each other.

**Palette** – A flat surface for mixing paint on. Wood, glass, plastic or metal surfaces can be used as palettes.

**Papier mâché** – Small pieces of paper mixed with glue or paste, which can be moulded when wet. See pages 134 and 136.

**Paste** – To glue or stick.

**Perspective** – The effect of creating three-dimensional space and depth on a flat surface.

**Pinching** – A method of working with clay by pinching it between your fingers and thumb to create hollowed-out forms. Pinch pots are made in this way.

**Plasticity** – Soft solid materials which have plasticity can be easily moulded or modelled into another shape e.g. clay.

**Portfolio** – A portable folder or case for carrying flat artworks.

**Portrait** – An artwork which depicts the likeness of a person. Portraits usually show the head and shoulders only but they can also include the whole body.

**Positive spaces** – The solid shapes and forms in an artwork.

**Primary colours** – Red, yellow and blue are primary colours. These are pure colours which cannot be made by mixing other colours.

**Prime** – To prepare a canvas or wall for painting by giving it an undercoat.

**Printing** – The process of transferring an image from one surface to another.

**Printing plate** – A flat surface which has a relief design on it. During the printing process, the relief design is inked and then transferred onto another surface. A printing plate is sometimes call a printing block.

**Proportion** – The relationship between the sizes of different parts of an image.

**Props** – Objects used in theatre or puppet shows e.g. a telephone, a cup, a bicycle.

**Pull a print** – The action of transferring an image from a printing plate onto a piece of paper or fabric.

**Puppet** – A figure or doll which is made to perform for an audience.

**Raffia** – A natural straw-like fibre, often used to make mats.

**Ready-made image** – An image which has been printed commercially e.g. a photograph of a person in a magazine.

**Relief** – A relief surface is uneven – some parts are raised and other parts are low.

**Relief printing** – Printing from a surface which has relief e.g. from carved lino or wood.

**San** – The indigenous hunting and gathering people of southern Africa who had a long tradition of rock painting. Sometimes called Bushmen but this name is now regarded as derogatory.

**Scoring** – The action of scratching grooves into clay in order to join two pieces of clay together with slip. See page 147.

**Sculpture** – A three-dimensional artwork which can be viewed from all sides.

**Secondary colours** – Green, orange, and purple are secondary colours. They are made by mixing only two primary colours.

**Sketch** – A preliminary drawing, usually done quite quickly.

**Slabbing** – Constructing three-dimensional forms by joining flat slabs of clay.

**Slip** – Clay mixed with a little water so that it is liquid. Slip is used to join pieces of clay. See page 147.

**Spontaneous** – Free, not pre-planned.

**Starch** – Laundry starch, used to stiffen material.

**Stencil** – A cut-out shape, usually made from cardboard. A stencil is placed on paper or fabric, then the surrounding area is painted or inked. When the stencil is removed, its unpainted shape exists on the paper or fabric. You can also trace around the edges of a stencil.

**Stipple** – A drawn or painted texture made up of tiny dots.

**Subject matter** – The content of an artwork e.g. a landscape, a portrait, a still life.

**Symbol** – A visual image or sign which represents something or somebody by association.

**Symmetry** – A design which has symmetry is perfectly balanced. Elements on both sides of an imaginary centre line of the design are the same.

**Technique** – The method of using particular art materials and tools.

**Tertiary colours** – Colours which are mixed using all three primary colours.

**Texture** – The surface feeling of an artwork, object, person or animal.

**Three-dimensional** – A three-dimensional form is not flat. It occupies space and has volume. It can be seen from all sides e.g. a sculpture or a pot.

**Tonal contrast** – This refers to the difference between tones. Tonal contrast is used for emphasis in an artwork.

**Tonal gradation chart** – A chart which shows a range of different shades of grey or of one colour.

**Tone** – The degree of lightness or darkness.

**Turpentine** – A liquid made from the resin of trees. It can dissolve oil-based ink or paint and it is used to remove these materials from surfaces.

**Two-dimensional** – A two-dimensional artwork has a flat surface e.g. a drawing, a painting, a print.

**Varnish** – A transparent liquid solution used to coat the surface of an artwork in order to protect it.

**Visualising** – Imagining, creating visual images in the mind.

**Volume** – The amount of space occupied by a three-dimensional form.

**Warm colours** – Colours which give off a feeling of warmth e.g. reds, oranges, yellows.

**Waste materials** – Discarded materials which have been thrown away e.g. used bus tickets, old scraps of leather, litter, fabric offcuts.

**Wedging** – The action of kneading clay to remove air bubbles from it and to create an even consistency.

**Woodcut** – A print made from a relief design carved onto a block of wood.

## Acknowledgements for photographs and illustrations

### For photographs:

Gillian Cargill, portrait of Helen Sebidi, page 14.

Lovell Friedman, pages 154, 155, 158.

Pierre Hinch, pages 78-80, 82-89, 92, 96, 98, 99, 102, 103, 115, 130, 133, 135, 138, 139-144, 146, 149, 153, 174, 188.

Annette Laubscher, pages 108, 109.

Gideon Mendel, pages 12-17, 21, 23, 24, 25, 32, 47, 136-138, 151, 153, 160, 162, 165, 166, 167, 169, 171, 172, 180, 181.

Justin Mthembu, page 91.

### For illustrations:

Adrian Kohler, page 177.

Wandile Mlangeni, pages 118, 119.

Tanki Mokhele, pages 38, 54, 148, 149, 159, 175, 176, 178, 180.

Charlotte Schaer, pages 26, 27, 29, 30, 42, 128, 156, 161, 164, 178.

Sydney Selepe, pages 146, 147, 148, 150, 152, 156, 157.

Members of the End Conscription Campaign helped to paint the colour on the children's mural at PROSCESS children's home.